Polygamy:
Polygyny, Polyandry, and Polyamory

By Daniel Young, Sarah Young, and Kate Young

Daniel Young, Sarah Young, and Kate Young

Polygamy:

Polygyny, Polyandry, and Polyamory

Fifth Estate

Blountsville, AL 35031

First Edition

Cover Designed by An Quigley

Printed on acid-free paper

Library of Congress Control No: 2013939967

ISBN: 9781936533367

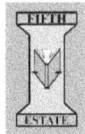

Fifth Estate, 2013

Daniel Young, Sarah Young, and Kate Young

TABLE OF CONTENTS

The Spiritual Side 7

Definitions 9

Patterns of Religions Worldwide 20

Modern practice..33

Secular Polygamy 48

Polygamy by Country..51

Looking at the Numbers 60

History 70

Coming Into The Present...94

Polygamy – A Social Choice......................................101

Compartments of the Heart 110

How to Choose a Wife (or Husband) 110

The God of Polygamy 120

Polygamy / Polygyny – How it Works........................134

Why Would You Want To?...138

Sex 163

The Logistics of Running Poly Households................166

Home and Housing..172

Resources – Time is Money 173

Downfalls and Traps - The Undoing 183

U.S. State Laws 190

Celibacy 195

Conclusion..217

Daniel Young, Sarah Young, and Kate Young

The Spiritual Side

"Our wretched species is so made that those who walk on the well-trodden path always throw stones at those who are showing a new road."
Voltaire

Among consenting adults, family should be a matter of choice and the configuration thereof should be the choice of the family members.

At the writing of this book, according to several sources, there are between 50,000 and 100,000 families in the U.S. living in polygamy (polygyny) today. Around half of those families are in the state of Utah alone. The number of people living in some form of polygamy in the U.S. was estimated at only 30,000 just five years ago. The numbers for polygamy alone have begun to climb rapidly, add to those the number who practice other forms of "poly" unions and the numbers begin to demand notice. This information could eclipse two other points, which in time will become far more important.

The first data point is this: The fastest growing religion in the U.S. is "none". These are people who consider themselves to be spiritual people but who claim no religion or denomination.

These are individuals searching for greater understanding and happiness beyond the confines of established religious or social constructs.

The second, more hidden data point is: The fastest growing population practicing polygamous marriages is not related to or based on religion. They are secular polygamists. If these two data points continue to grow the institution of polygamy will become a social force in the U.S. within the next generation. It will become impossible to reject polygamy as a religious throwback of a few fundamental radicals. Polygamy will become part of society, practiced by the religious, spiritual, and secular alike.

People will search for and find their own happiness, and when enough have done, so they will have a voice loud enough to change the laws of the land. The gay and lesbian movement has exemplified this. Polygamy and plural marriage may be the next movement in the search for individual freedom and happiness.

There are various forms of polygamy and plural marriages, which need to be defined before we begin.

Definitions

Polygamy is used as a general term and exists in three specific forms: Polygyny, Polyandry, and Polyamory

Polygamy: The act of having more than one spouse. A husband having more than one wife or wife having more than one husband is called polygamy. This is a general term, which has come to mean the same as polygyny, which is a more specific term.

Polygyny: When a man has multiple simultaneous wives, the state is specifically called polygyny. You will also hear the term, "Plural Marriage" or "Celestial Marriage" used by the FLDS church when one husband has several wives.

Polyandry: When a woman has multiple simultaneous husbands it is specifically called polyandry.

Polyamory: Group marriage, where the family unit consists of multiple husbands and multiple wives, is specifically called polyamory.

Historically, all three practices have been found, but polygyny, the marriage or commitment between one man and several women, is by far the most common. Confusion arises when the broad term "polygamy" is used when a specific form of plural marriage is being referenced.

Within the context of polygamy, it is polygyny that has spread throughout the world, being propagated by the vehicles of religion, state, culture, and the heart's desire.

Here, we must pause and think about how we view the boundaries of polygyny. Is the institution defined as a man having two wives? Most people practicing this type of marriage are legally married to only one woman. The other wives are taken in a spiritual marriage or a heart-felt commitment. In the civil courts the second marriage does not exist, unless it is viewed in the same way as common-law marriages. Is it considered polygyny if a married man keeps a woman as a lover? Does he have to support her? If a man marries two women in separate towns and neither are aware of the arrangement is that polygyny? In the U.S. that arrangement is termed bigamy and the perpetrator is far more likely to be prosecuted, since it is seen as a violation of state and federal laws. If one considers situations wherein a wife is unaware her husband supports a lover or mistress, to whom he is committed the number of polygyny cases would be amazingly high.

According to the *Journal of Couple and Relationship Therapy*, approximately 50 percent of married women and 60 percent of married men will have an extramarital affair at some time in their marriage. And since it is unlikely that the people having affairs are married to each other in every case, the current statistics on the percentage of married couples who cheat on each other means that someone is having an affair in nearly 80 percent of marriages. Most of these cannot be considered polygyny because of the brevity of the encounters. So, for clarification we will consider polygyny as an arrangement where a man is committed to the well being, financial, physical, sexual, and emotional support of two or more women. Polygyny is what people think of when polygamy is mentioned. It has by far the highest occurrence of all "poly" lifestyles. For this reason we will spend more time examining it. When it comes to the sections on the logistics of running polygamist households the information easily translates for other poly households if one assumes that most women are as likely to work as men.

Polyandry

Polyandry is a practice where a woman has more than one husband at the same time. Fraternal polyandry was traditionally practiced among nomadic Tibetans in Nepal, parts of China and part of northern India, in which two or more brothers are married to the same wife, with her having equal sexual access and responsibility to them. Polyandry is believed to be more likely in societies with scarce environmental resources, as it is believed to limit human population growth and enhance survival of the unit and especially the children. It is a rare form of marriage that exists not only among poor families, but also the elite.

Polyamory

Polyamory is a more difficult state to define. It can be a fluid situation where partners within a marriage have partners outside the marriage with the consent of all. A man will have a lover and his wife will have a lover, all with mutual consent and approval. This is usually referred to as an open marriage. In the true sense, Polyamory is the combining of married couples. It can also be one of the most stable states with two or more married couples in turn committing to the other married couples, sharing mates and resources.

Seattle, Washington seems to be the "poly" capital of the U.S. in many ways. In an article in the publication, "Seattle City Living," by Alberto Lacao Jr. the subject of Polyamory in the U.S. is explored. The article reads in part:

Polyamory is a relationship model in which a person has more than one intimate relationship with the knowledge of everyone involved. Unlike polygamy or polyandry, in which a person has multiple spouses (and which usually has religious connotations to it), those who practice polyamory are free to have other romantic partners.

Matt Bullen and his wife, Vee (not her real name), who live in Southeast Seattle, opened their relationship more than five years ago while they were living abroad. For half of each week, she left their rural town to stay in a city several hours away for work.

"One night, we were talking, and I asked the question, 'We're a responsible couple; we're both apart a lot and under ongoing stress. What would happen if one of us found someone for company for one night?'" Matt explained. "Not out of desperation, but just hypothetical. Vee wasn't interested, but we agreed to it."

Matt and Vee didn't act on their new agreement until their family returned to Seattle in 2009. They made friends with three people who were all in a polyamorous relationship, and their interest in polyamory developed from there.

A polyamorous family

Emma (not her real name), who has been dating Matt for the last 16 months, said she felt nothing odd with the arrangement. "I was actually pretty surprised with how everything was normal," she said. "'Normal' is the only word you can use to describe it."

She attends the Bullens' son Edwin's soccer games on the weekends, and Edwin (not his real name) sees her like an "auntie."

Emma, who enjoys her independence, found this relationship fit perfectly and considers herself monogamous. "I date Matt and have no other interest in dating anyone else," she said. "The dynamics work out well for me. I get my time and then relationship time." There is no set template for the structure of a poly relationship. Like Matt, Vee and Emma's arrangement, there are triads involving three people, or quads involving four people, group marriages...the list goes on.

There are many misconceptions of what polyamory is and what it is not. Many may assume that polyamory is the same as an open relationship or even swinging. Polyamory is centered on the actual relationships more than sexual contact.

According to Allena Gabosch, executive director for the Center of Sex Positive Culture in Seattle. She acknowledged, "There's a bit of controversy about what 'polyamory' means to those of us who are poly. We get to define it, and we all define it differently. For many, poly puts the emphasis on 'loving, intimate relationships,' where[as] 'open' may be more about casual sexual encounters. That said, I know many poly folk who practice both."

As for her relationships, Vee makes it clear that her relationships "are not a causal thing. We truly love each other, and if something happened to the other one, we are there for each other. Our relationships are like friends with benefits but long-term."

One thing all emphasized is that polyamory is not cheating. As in a monogamous relationship, infidelity or any other dishonesty is not tolerated.

"In cheating," Emma pointed out, "there is a fundamental dishonesty involved that really doesn't exist in a healthy poly relationship."
Matt explained, "Cheating is not poly. If that's an excuse to use to cheat, it will not work."

The New Relationship Wave?

Matt believes that the next wave of polyamory being more socially acceptable will be "those who are currently poly but who camouflage it, will finally stop it. They will come out and say that, 'You know what? This picture on my desk at work is not my sister or brother, but my other partner.' Because they had found a second or third partner and are sick of disguising it."

Polyamory and other forms of multi-partner relationships are nothing new. There was a large devotion to open marriage during the free-love movement of the '60s and '70s — that dropped during the AIDS scare of the 1980s. Thanks to the boom of the Internet in the 1990s, polyamory started to emerge as a social movement.

The long run?

According to Pepper Schwartz, professor of sociology at the University of Washington, not enough studies have been done on polyamory to know its actual viability. "Polyamory is a much more complicated form of living together for people who have not grown up with a village or [are] living in a group mentality," she said. "Not impossible, just difficult. Even in those societies where multiple forms of marriage are legal and culturally familiar, the anthropological literature is replete with tales of competition, jealousy and favoritism. So I do not see it as a new trend but something that a small group of people will want and an even smaller group of people will be able to do successfully."

Vee agrees about the uncertainty, but she points out that it is "no different from a monogamous relationship, with a 50-percent chance of divorce. If you ask that about every mono relationship, people would be paralyzed." (end of excerpts)

Group marriage

Polyamory also take the form of two or more families which commit to a type of interrelated marriage or group marriage. Polyamory, or group marriage is a marriage where the family unit consists of more than one man and more than one woman, any of whom share parental responsibility for any children arising from the marriages. Group marriage is a form of non-monogamy consisting of multiple households or multiple marriages converging into a single support system, providing emotional, sexual, financial, and physical support and resources to the members of the group.

Another possibility, which has been conceived in fiction (notably in Robert Heinlein's *The Moon Is a Harsh Mistress*), is a line marriage, where a deceased or departing spouse in the group is continually replaced by another so that family property never becomes dispersed through inheritance.

Polygamy

The general term of Polygamy is used to define a practice where a man has more than one wife at the same time. Although the specific term for this practice is polygyny, we will follow the common usage here and use the terms interchangeably. When polyandry or polyamory is discussed we will define or identify those states separately.

Polygamy / Polygyny have existed since recorded history and have been practiced throughout the ancient Near East, the Far East, the Mediterranean empires, Europe and Britain. Royal archives of Kings and Caesars and writings of ancient historians such as Moses, Herodotus, Demosthenes, Polybius, Strabo, Livy, Plutarch, Tacitus, Suetonius and Josephus attest to this. Besides legitimate marriage, temple prostitution and the spoils of war were the two most common sources of women for men of the time, but these cannot be considered as polygamous relationships since there was no enduring commitment.

Records of explorers and missionaries in the Christian era confirmed the widespread practice of polygamy among native tribes in Africa and the Americas.

Several conditions may have precipitated the marital status and family structure. Polygamy was likely to have occurred in societies where warfare, famine, or other conditions depleted the number of available males. Those who survived warfare or were victors were considered more desirable mates. In certain religions, beliefs and guidelines urge followers to take more than one wife. The wives produce children, who are brought up in the religion of the father, promoting rapid growth of that particular religion. Thus, a country or government may encourage polygamy to repopulate. A religion may encourage polygamy to increase its numbers. A society may condone polygamy to better secure its continuation. Then, there is polygamy that occurs simply as a matter of the heart, where people wish to live together out of love and respect. Each of these has occurred and continues to occur in every nation in various forms.

In the United States, where there are laws forbidding polygamy, there are well over 100,000 people risking arrest and prison by following their heart or faith. Across the globe the history, reasons, and practices vary immensely, but in every region of the planet, it continues.

There are three forces affecting the course of relationships: Religion, Culture, and Personal choice.

Patterns of Religions Worldwide

According to the *Ethnographic Atlas Codebook*, of 1231 societies noted, 186 were monogamous. 453 had occasional polygamy, 588 had more frequent polygamy, and 4 had polyandry. At the same time, even within societies which allow polygamy, the actual practice of polygamy occurs relatively rarely. There are exceptions: in Senegal, for example, nearly 47 percent of marriages are multiple.

To take on more than one wife often requires considerable resources: this may put polygamy beyond the means of the vast majority of people within those societies. Such appears the case in many traditional Islamic societies, and in Imperial China. Within polygynous (polygamous) societies, multiple wives often become a status symbol denoting wealth, power, and fame. They were the "token wives."

The variety of practices is fascinating. It may help our general understanding to break down the history and various practices by religions and then by country or region. We will begin with an overview by religion.

Buddhism

In Buddhism, marriage is not a sacrament. It is purely a secular affair and the monks do not participate in it. Hence it receives no religious sanction. Forms of marriage consequently vary from country to country. It is said in the Parabhava Sutta that "a man who is not satisfied with one woman and seeks out other women is on the path to decline". Other fragments in the Buddhist scripture can be found that seem to treat polygamy unfavorably, leading some authors to conclude that Buddhism generally does not approve of it or alternatively that it is a tolerated, but inferior marital model.

Until 1935 polygamy was legally recognized in Thailand. In Burma, polygamy was also frequent. It is still legally recognized but very rarely practiced in modern day and is socially less acceptable in Burma. In Sri Lanka, polyandry was practiced (though not widespread) till recent times. When the Buddhist texts were translated into Chinese, concubines were added to the list of inappropriate partners. In Tibet polyandry as well as polygamy (having several wives or husbands) was never regarded as having sex with inappropriate partners.

Tibet is home to the largest and most flourishing polyandrous community in the world today. Most typically, fraternal polyandry is practiced, but sometimes father and son have a common wife, which is a unique family structure in the world. Other forms of marriage are also present, like group marriage and monogamous marriage. Polyandry (especially fraternal polyandry) is also common among Buddhists in Bhutan, Ladakh, and other parts of the Indian subcontinent.

Hinduism

Polygamy was practiced in many sections of Hindu society in ancient times. The Hindu god, Lord Krishna, the 8th incarnation of the Hindu god Vishnu had 16,108 wives at his kingdom in Dwarka.

Marriage laws in India are dependent upon the religion of the subject in question. Although the Vedas and the Hindu religion itself do not outlaw polygamy, the laws under the Hindu Marriage Act have deemed polygamy to be illegal for Hindus, Jains, Buddhists, and Sikhs. Only Muslim men in India are allowed to have multiple wives, since they are governed under Sharia law.

Islam

Polygamy is allowed in Islam with specific limitations. A man can have no more than four wives at any one time, although those who can afford more wives, such as rulers and the wealthy, often have more wives than the Qur'an suggests.

The Qur'an clearly states that men who choose this route must deal with their wives justly. This is very much like the laws set down for Jewish men. If the husband fears that he cannot deal with his wives justly, then he should only marry one. Islamic scholars teach that the husband must tell the first wife if he wants to marry another. A husband doesn't necessarily need the permission of his first wife, but the first wife has the right to divorce if the husband re-marries without her liking. Women, on the other hand, are only allowed to marry one husband, although they are allowed to remarry after a divorce. Although many Muslim countries retain traditional Islamic Law, which permits polygamy, others have chosen to follow more secular laws, which do not condone polygamy. Azerbaijan, Bosnia and Herzegovina, Tunisia and Turkey prohibit polygamy.

According to traditional Islamic law, a man may take up to four wives, and each of those wives must have her own property, assets, and dowry. Usually the wives have little to no contact with each other and lead separate, individual lives in their own houses, and sometimes in different cities, though they all share the same husband, each having knowledge that he is married to other women.

As the Qur'an indicates (4:3), the issue of polygamy in Islam is understood in the light of community obligations towards orphans and widows. Islam, as a universal religion that is suitable for all times and places, cannot ignore these compelling obligations.

The basic principle in Islam is that men are held responsible for their behavior towards women just as women are responsible for their behavior towards men.

In the modern Islamic world, polygamy is mainly found in Saudi Arabia, West and East Africa. In Sudan it is encouraged by the president because the female population is high. This points back to one of the main social pressures bringing about polygamy when war has decimated the male population.

Among the 22 member states of the Arab League, Tunisia alone explicitly prohibits polygamy. In many of the more secularized Arab countries, such as Egypt and Lebanon polygamy is frowned upon. Other countries including Libya, Pakistan, and Morocco require the written permission of the first wife if her husband wishes to marry a second, third, or fourth wife.

It should be noted that the idea of four being the limit of wives has to do with only one interpretation and application of Islam.

Judaism

Multiple marriage was considered a realistic alternative in the case of famine, widowhood, or female infertility like in the practice of levirate marriage, wherein a man was required to marry and support his deceased brother's widow, as mandated by Deuteronomy 25:5–10. The practice was prevalent in the Torah. The purpose was to raise up children in the name of the deceased brother in order to continue his name, lineage and inheritance. Scholars believe that polygamy was widely practiced in the biblical era, especially in Old Testament times. The practice began to decline, not because the practice was revoked but because it required a significant amount of wealth to carry out. Later, as Rome began to enforce its customs as laws the state would make it difficult to have more than one wife, although mistresses were tolerated.

The Torah includes a few specific regulations on the practice of polygamy, such as Exodus 21:10, which states that multiple marriages are not to diminish the status of the first wife, (specifically, her right to food, clothing and conjugal relations). Deuteronomy 17:17 states that the king shall not have too many wives. The monogamy of the Roman Empire and its control and influence over the Jews may have been one of the causes of the diminishing view of polygamy. The social difference between the Romans and the Jews was the cause of two entries in the writings of Josephus describing how the polygamous marriages of Herod were permitted under Jewish custom.

Polygamy in Judaism

Polygamy existed among the Israelites before the time of Moses, who continued the institution without imposing any limit on the number of marriages a Hebrew husband could enter into.

The Jewish Encyclopedia states, "While there is no evidence of a polyandrous state in primitive Jewish society, polygamy seems to have been a well-established institution, dating from ancient times and extending to comparatively modern days."

In later times, the Talmud, the body of Jewish civil and ceremonial law and legend comprising the Mishnah and the Gemara, restricted the number by the ability of the husband to maintain the wives properly. Some rabbis, however, counseled that a man should not take more than four wives. Polygamy was prohibited in Judaism by the rabbis, not God. Rabbi Gershom ben Judah is credited by forbidding polygamy in the 11th century outlawing it for a 1,000 years, a time frame that ended in 1987. His proclamation was directed to the Eastern European Jews, the Ashkanazi. The Mediterranean or

Sephardic Jews continued to practice polygamy, believing the Rabbi did not have the authority to change divine order.

Will Durant, the author of "The Story of Civilization" states; "polygamy was practiced by rich Jews in Islamic lands, but was rare among the Jews of Christendom." According to Joseph Ginat, professor of social and culture anthropology at the University of Haifa, polygamy is common and growing among the 180,000 Bedouin of Israel. Polygamy is becoming more common among Mediterranean Jews living in Yemen, where rabbis permit Jews to marry up to four wives. In modern Israel, where a wife cannot bear children or is mentally ill, the rabbis give a husband the right to marry a second woman without divorcing his first wife. This is in accordance with Jewish custom and provides the husband with needed support while he takes care of the first wife. They did not make provisions for polyandry if the husband were ill or unfit.

While it could be argued, in a purely esoteric view, that God made one man and one women as the perfect model of marriage, before man was ejected from the Garden of Eden, either literally or metaphorically, he began killing his fellow man. In a land of war and death the number of men decreased to the point of societal collapse. Thus, two separate systems emerged. Polygamy and a religious welfare system served to provide for the widows and orphans.

The arrangement for widows and orphans functioned, as ours
does today, mostly for the lower economic class. Jewish women
could and did inherit land, property, and money. An eldest
female or only child could stand to inherit the estate of a
parent. Middle and upper class Jewish women were powerful
and independent forces in families and communities. Wealthy
women were the ones funding the ministry of Jesus. Women
could be upwardly mobile, but for those women and children
left, bereft and penniless, with no resources or hope of
resources, the system did not supply any way to escape living
in subsistence, again, much like our dole of today.

People desire a home and hearth of their own. No one wishes
to live, not knowing where they will sleep or raise their child.
Marriage was the only way for women to obtain consistent
food, shelter, clothing, and a chance for their children to inherit
position or land. Polygamy, under the social conditions of class
and poverty, was the better path for women.

The church father Justin Martyr mentions that in his time
Jewish men were permitted to have four or five wives.

History records the story of Babatha, who was a Jewish woman and a second wife. The record is interesting since it reveals much about the status of middle and upper class women of the time.

In 1960, archeologist Yigael Yadin discovered a leather pouch containing personal documents of a woman in a cave, which came to be known as the Cave of Letters, located near the Dead Sea. The documents found include legal contracts concerning marriage, property transfers, and guardianship, ranging in dates from 96 to 134 AD. The documents depicted a vivid picture of life for a middle class to upper class Jewish woman during that time.

Babatha was born in approximately 104 CE in Maoza. She lived in the port town of Maoza in what is now modern day Jordan at beginning of the 2nd century CE. She was likely the only child or eldest daughter since she inherited her father's date palm orchard upon her parents' deaths.

By 124 CE, she had been married and widowed with a young son, Jesus. The name, Jesus, was a very common name and more than one with that name was crucified. There was even more than one claiming to be the anointed one. Her son was not one of those. As far as we know he was an average child. By 125 CE Babatha was remarried to Judah, owner of three date palm orchards in the town of Ein Gedi (an oasis and town situated west of the Dead Sea). Judah already had a wife. Judah's other wife had a teenage daughter. It is uncertain whether Babatha lived in the same home as the first wife or if Judah traveled between two separate households, as polygamy was still allowed in the Jewish community.

The documents found in leather pouch offer information and insight concerning this marriage and her status in the relationship. In their marriage contract, Judah's debts become part of her liability, indicating a financial equality. In other words, Babatha was responsible for paying off her husband's debts if he were to die, become injured, or for some other reason could not pay.

In 128 CE, a legal document shows that Judah took a loan without interest from Babatha, showing that she had control of her own money despite the union. Now Judah was financially indebted to Babatha. Upon Judah's death in 130 CE, she seized his estates in Ein Gedi as a guarantee for payment against his debts, which she had covered through her loan to him, as stated in the marriage contract.

Another document of importance concerned the guardianship of Babatha's son. In 125 CE, Babatha brought a lawsuit to court against the appointed guardians of her orphaned son, citing their insufficient disbursement of funds. The document contains Babatha's petition that full guardianship responsibility of her son and his property be transferred to her control.

This is amazing insight into the range and depth of the place of Jewish women within polygamist marriages in the Jewish community at the time of the second century. We can assume it reflects marriage in general in that socio-economic class. But Jewish polygamy began to clash with Roman monogamy at the time of the early church and was eventually pushed out by way of newly established civil laws and social pressure.

When the Christian Church came into being, polygamy was still practiced by the Jews. We find few direct references to it in the New Testament. From this some have inferred that occurrences must have decreased, and that the Jewish people had become monogamous, but the conclusion appears to be unwarranted and skewed by incorrect interpretation. Josephus, in two places in his writings, speaks of polygamy as a recognized institution. Justin Martyr makes it a matter of reproach to Trypho that the Jewish teachers permitted a man to have several wives. Indeed when in 212 A.D. the "lex Antoniana de civitate" gave the rights of Roman Citizenship to great numbers of Jews, it was found necessary to tolerate polygamy among them, even though it was against Roman law for a citizen to have more than one wife. In 285 A.D. a constitution of Diocletian and Maximian forbade polygamy to all subjects of the empire without exception. But with the Jews, at least, the enactment failed and in 393 A.D. a special law was issued by Theodosius to compel the Jews to relinquish this national custom, but they did not conform.

Polygamy was not banned in the Jewish community until about 1000CE by Rabbi Gershom, a leading rabbi born in France. This, it was said, was to avoid persecution of the Jews arising from their variance from the social and legal norms in Europe at the time. Anti-Semitism was running unchecked and the good Rabbi was trying to protect his people by forcing them to fit in to the society and become less identifiable as "different" or "Jewish."

Modern practice

In the modern day, Rabbinic Judaism has essentially outlawed polygamy. Ashkenazi Jews have followed Rabbenu Gershom's ban since the 11th century. Some Sephardi and Mizrahi Jews (particularly those from Yemen and Iran) continue the practice of polygamy in those countries where it is legal.

Israel has made new polygamist marriages illegal. Provisions were instituted to allow for existing polygamous families emigrating from countries where the practice was legal. Furthermore, former chief rabbi Ovadia Yosef and Israeli columnist Greer Fay Cashman have come out in favor of legalizing polygamy and the practice of pilegesh (concubine).

Among Karaite Jews, who do not adhere to Rabbinic interpretations of the Torah, polygamy is almost non-existent today. Like other Jews, Karaites interpret Leviticus 18:18 to mean that a man can only take a second wife if his first wife gives her consent (Keter Torah on Leviticus, pp. 96–97) and Karaites interpret Exodus 21:10 to mean that a man can only take a second wife if he is capable of maintaining the same level of marital duties due to his first wife. The marital duties are food, clothing, and sexual gratification. Because of these biblical limitations and because most countries outlaw it, polygamy is considered highly impractical, and there are only a few known cases of it among Karaite Jews today.

Christianity

The New Testament does not specifically address the morality of polygamy. 1 Timothy, however, states that certain Church leaders should have but one wife: "A *bishop* then must be blameless, the husband of one wife, vigilant, sober, of good behavior, given to hospitality, apt to teach" (chapter 3, verse 2; see also verse 12 regarding deacons having only one wife). Similar counsel is repeated in the first chapter of Titus. The admonition to have one wife is not, as some would have us believe, an edict against divorce, but an observation that a man married to multiple wives would not have time or resources to minister to members of a church and his extended family.

In modern times a minority of Roman Catholic theologians have argued that polygamy, though not ideal, can be a legitimate form of Christian marriage in certain regions, in particular Africa.

Periodically, Christian reform movements that have aimed at rebuilding Christian doctrine based on the Bible alone (*sola scriptura*) have at least temporarily accepted polygamy as a

Biblical practice. For example, during the Protestant Reformation, in a document referred to simply as "Der Beichtrat" (or "*The Confessional Advice*"), Martin Luther granted the Landgrave Philip of Hesse, who, for many years, had been living "constantly in a state of adultery and fornication," a dispensation to take a second wife. The double marriage was to be done in secret however, to avoid public scandal. Some fifteen years earlier, in a letter to the Saxon Chancellor Gregor Bruck, Luther stated that he could not "forbid a person to marry several wives, for it does not contradict Scripture." ("*Ego sane fateor, me non posse prohibere, si quis plures velit uxores ducere, nec repugnat sacris literis.*")

"On February 14, 1650, the parliament at Nürnberg decreed that, because so many men were killed during the Thirty Years' War, the churches for the following ten years could not admit any man under the age of 60 into a monastery. Priests and ministers not bound by any monastery were allowed to marry. Lastly, the decree stated that every man was allowed to marry up to ten women. The men were admonished to behave honorably, provide for their wives properly, and prevent animosity among them."

In Sub-Saharan Africa, there has often been a tension between the Christian churches' insistence on monogamy and traditional polygamy. In recent times there have been moves for accommodation; in other instances, churches have resisted such moves strongly. African Independent Churches have sometimes referred to those parts of the Old Testament, which describe polygamy in defending the practice.

Latter Day Saint movement

The history of Mormon polygamy began with Joseph Smith, Jr. receiving a revelation on July 17, 1831 that some Mormon men who were specifically commanded to do so would practice "plural marriage." This was later published in the Doctrine and Covenants of the LDS Church).

Despite Smith's revelation, the 1835 edition of the 101st Section of the Doctrine and Covenants, written after the doctrine of plural marriage began to be practiced, publicly condemned polygamy. In 1850 this scripture was used by John Taylor to quiet rumors in Liverpool, England of Mormon polygamy.

Polygamy was made illegal in the state of Illinois during the 1839–44 Nauvoo era when several top Mormon leaders, including Smith, Brigham Young and Heber C. Kimball, took plural wives. Mormon elders who publicly taught that all men were commanded to enter plural marriage were subject to harsh discipline. On June 7, 1844 the Nauvoo Expositor criticized Smith for plural marriage. After Joseph Smith's murder by a mob on June 27, 1844, the main body of Mormons left Nauvoo and followed Brigham Young to Utah where the practice of plural marriage continued.

The waffling of the church on the subject of polygamy, or as they term it, plural marriage, seems to be centered around the political and social pressures against polygamy in conservative America. The explanation of the modern LDS church regarding the purpose of polygamy is to point to the persecution of male members and thus the decline of the number of men in the newly formed LDS Church. The writings of Joseph Smith do not seem to bear this out. The first or primary reason for the doctrine was based on the effort to re-establish pure and historical biblical doctrine, seeing as how polygamy was never spoken against in the New Testament. However, it did not decrease Smith's urgency to establish the doctrine. Some argue this was a divine unction while others are skeptical since he had been caught in affairs several times.

In 1852 Brigham Young, the second president of the LDS Church publicly acknowledged the practice of plural marriage through a sermon he gave. Additional sermons by top Mormon leaders on the virtues of polygamy followed. Controversy followed when polygamy became a social cause, writers began to publish works condemning polygamy. The key plank of the 1856 Republican Party platform was "to prohibit in the territories those twin relics of barbarism, polygamy and slavery". In 1862, Congress issued the Morill Anti-Bigamy act, which clarified that the practice of polygamy was illegal in all US territories. The LDS Church believed that their religiously-based practice of plural marriage (polygamy/polygyny) was protected by the United States Constitution. However, the 1878 Supreme Court voted in unison in the case of *Reynolds v. United States* and declared that polygamy was not protected by the Constitution. This was based on the longstanding legal principle that "laws are made for the government of actions, and while they cannot interfere with mere religious belief and opinions, they may with practices."

Anti-polygamy legislation in the U.S. led some Mormons to immigrate to Canada and Mexico. In 1890, LDS Church president Wilford Woodruff issued a public declaration announcing that the LDS Church had discontinued new plural marriages. The banning of an action by the authorities does not mean the populace will follow. The Smoot Hearing in 1904, documented that the LDS Church members continued practicing polygamy. The uprising from Congress and non-Mormons spurred the LDS Church to issue another Manifesto claiming that it had ceased performing new plural marriages.

In an act of self-preservation in 1910 the LDS Church began excommunicating those who entered into, or performed, new plural marriages. Even so, many plural husbands and wives continued to cohabit until their deaths. The last documented mainstream LDS polygamous marriage was the grandfather of current LDS apostle, Edward Eyring, and two distant cousins of Mitt Romney.

Fundamentalist Mormonism

Enforcement of the 1890 Manifesto caused various groups to leave the LDS Church. These groups believed polygamy was biblical and religiously correct and they were determined to continue the institution. Polygamy among these groups persists today in Utah and neighboring states as well as in Canada.

Polygamist churches of Mormon origin are often referred to as "Mormon fundamentalist" or **Fundamentalist Latter Day Saints (FLDS).** These churches are offshoots of the mainline Mormon church, though the LDS Church has disowned them.

The schism occurred because the revelation of Joseph Smith regarding plural marriage, or polygamy was rescinded by the church in order to become compliant with U.S. laws and allow Utah to become a state. At that time the group within the church broke away, maintaining that the law of God, as spoken through Smith, should be maintained over that of any government.

The religious basis of plural marriage came through a revelation to Joseph Smith that was written down in 1843, but it was apparently received by Smith and discussed with the church leaders prior to becoming doctrine. The commandment was the recreation of the marital order of the patriarchs of the Old Testament. Smith realized plural marriage, or polygyny, had never been stopped or changed in the Old or New Testaments. Thus they viewed plural marriage as sacred, giving it the title of "celestial marriage."

Fundamentalists cite the revelation of Joseph Smith on polygamy as a foundation but they also cite the 1886 revelation to John Taylor, the third president of the LDS Church, as the basis for their authority to continue the practice of plural marriage.

The revelation of John Taylor was written on Monday, 27 September 1886. It reads:

September 27, 1886

My son John: You have asked me concerning the New and

Everlasting Covenant and how far it is binding upon my people.

Thus saith the Lord All commandments that I give must be obeyed by those calling themselves by my name unless they are revoked by me or by my authority and how can I revoke an everlasting covenant.

For I the Lord am everlasting and my covenants cannot be abrogated nor done away with; but they stand forever.

Have I not given my word in great plainness on this subject?

Yet have not great numbers of my people been negligent in the observance of my law and the keeping of my commandment, and yet have I borne with them these many years and this because of their weakness because of the perilous times. And furthermore it is more pleasing to me that men should use their free agency in regard to these matters.

Nevertheless I the Lord do not change and my word and my covenants and my law do not.

And as I have heretofore said by my servant Joseph all those who would enter into my glory must and shall obey my law.

And have I not commanded men that if they were Abraham's seed and would enter into my glory they must do the works of Abraham.

I have not revoked this law nor will I for it is everlasting and those who will enter into my glory must obey the conditions thereof, even so Amen.

A fundamentalist author summed up the FLDS position: "In the revelation to John Taylor, dated September 27, 1886, the Lord said that he had not, could not and would not revoke the Law of Abraham which is Plural Marriage."

Black Muslims in the U.S.

In a recent interview conducted by Barbara Bradley Hagerty on National Public Radio on May 28, 2008, polygamy among Black Muslims was discussed. Excerpts of the interview follow:

Polygamy in the U.S. is not limited to remote enclaves in the West or breakaway sects once affiliated with the Mormon Church. Several scholars say it's growing among black Muslims in the inner city — and particularly in Philadelphia, which is known for its large orthodox black Muslim community.

Take Zaki and Mecca, who have been married for nearly 12 years. In their late 20s, they live in the Philadelphia suburbs, have a 5-year-old son and own a real estate business.

Zaki also has something else: a second wife.
Two years ago, Mecca told her husband she wanted to study Arabic in the Middle East, which would mean a lot of time away from home.

"We were talking about it," Mecca recalls, "and the first thing that came to my mind was, 'I'm going to have to find you another wife!'"

Zaki was game. After all, he had been raised in a polygamous home in Philadelphia. Like many black Muslims, his father subscribed to an orthodox view of Islam that allows a man to marry several women. Zaki says he loved having seven siblings and four mothers, especially at dinnertime.

"I would find out who's making what that particular night. I know that this mom makes barbequed chicken better than my other mom makes fried chicken, so I'm going with the barbequed chicken tonight. Things of that nature," he says with a laugh.

Unlike Zaki, Mecca was raised by a single mother and converted from Southern Baptist to Muslim when she was 16.

Mecca launched a nationwide search. She found candidates by word of mouth. She scoured the Internet. Eventually, she interviewed about a dozen women.

"I had to make sure that she'd be the right fit — not just for my husband, but for our whole family," Mecca says.

But the ultimate match was right under their noses: 20-year-old Aminah, who was a friend of Zaki's younger sister. Aminah knew Mecca was looking for a second wife but thought she was too young. That is, until one night after a dinner party when Mecca pulled her aside. Mecca asked Aminah if she would consider marrying Zaki.

"And I said, 'That's funny, because I was thinking the same thing,'" Aminah says.

Zaki was the last to know the identity of the final candidate to be his bride. He could have vetoed the choice, of course, but he was delighted.

In October 2007, he and Aminah married in a religious, not civil, ceremony. Many polygamous marriages are conducted in secret and are not legally binding because state laws prohibit them.

Zaki moves between homes (of the wives) on alternating nights. But every week after Friday prayers, they get together as a family.

"It can be a variety of things," Zaki says. "Going to a nice restaurant, catching a movie, going bowling, maybe seeing a concert. All kind of things."

"I always call it family date night, because it's one big date," Mecca says. "We just chill. I always look forward to it. We always have a ball, laughing, goofing around."

Islam requires that the husband treat each wife equally. Zaki explains that doesn't mean he gives them the same things. For example, Mecca likes jewelry but Aminah doesn't.

But, he says, "If I upgrade one, then I have to upgrade the other. But the upgrade may not be the same because you have two different women with two different tastes."

They've worked out a system. Even still, why would a woman want to share her husband?

"Well, I'm looking at it more as a spiritual perspective," Mecca says. "Zaki is a blessing — just like everything else. He is a loan from God, is the way I look at it. And in my religion, if he's able and capable to [marry another wife], I wouldn't want to hold him back. So, why not?"

She acknowledges that there have been "a few bumps in the road." But she hasn't once second-guessed sharing Zaki with Aminah.

Zaki believes ultimately, polygamy is good for society — especially in the inner city, where intact families are rare and many kids grow up without their fathers.

"There are a lot of blessings in it because you're helping legitimize and build a family that's rooted in values and commitment. And the children that come out of those types of relationships only become a benefit to society at large."
Many orthodox Muslims agree. You can find them on Fridays at a mosque in South Philadelphia.

Abdullah, the imam, has conducted religious ceremonies for a dozen polygamous marriages.
Abdullah says polygamy in Islam dates back to the 7th century, when battles were killing off Muslim men and leaving widows and children unprotected.

And while polygamy may seem like a man's paradise, Abdullah says, often an unmarried woman initiates it.

The N.P.R. interview goes on to point out the dearth of men in the inner city. Crime, killings, incarceration, H.I.V. and other problems have left countless women alone to raise children. They are unprotected and uncared for in a hostile environment. Some modern inner cities are compared to 7th century nations and battles mentioned prior. Polygamy was the solution then and it may be the solution now. The national social safety net can only do so much to provide for women and children.

Polygamy provides the father, husband and family structure missing in the equation.

Whether wars are from invading hordes or between gang members of the inner city, the same social pressures push societies to respond in similar ways to survive and internally balance.

We may see this take place in aging populations where more and more women are continuing to live longer than men and there are fewer prospects of marriage as women age past their 60's.

Secular Polygamy

The fastest growing division of polygamists are those who have no particular religious adherence to the belief or practice. They have instead stepped out of social confines and sought a way that is more suitable to their needs. There are many reasons one may choose polygamy and many configurations to that state of matrimony.

If one believes there may not be a "one and only" or perfect mate but instead a small group of people one can love and trust, it is natural to wish to find and hold onto those people. Sex may not be involved in some situations, where one wishes to commit to the wellbeing of a loving friend and help provide a better life to someone. Sex may be secondary while deep commitment is a primary motivation. One may argue this can be done without marriage but if marriage is commitment we are only talking semantics.

Indeed, it is my belief that polygamy will in time become an excepted mode of marriage within the next two or three generations.

There are valid reasons for my belief. Prior to the great world wars in the U.S. and up until the 1950's life in the U.S. was centered around a tight knit nuclear family. It extended family structure with members tasked with caring for their own elderly and infirmed. Then men left for war and women were forced into the work place. The wages of women were taxed and the government grew and consumed the extra income. When men came back from war many women kept their jobs and men came back into the job pool. The government rebalanced and again began to grow to consume the extra income in taxable wages. Taxes increased as government greed forced both parties to work for less realized income. The nuclear family began to dissolve.

Since there were no parents left at home to care for anyone and since people were forced to work to make ends meet they were left without aide or assistance in their old age and ill health. The government took the place of the family and set up a social safety net – Social Security – Medicare – Medicaid – Disability… But now the government has reached its limits because the people have reached their limits. Americans have worked harder and harder for longer and longer hours but their realized income adjusted for inflation has not gone up since the 1970's. There is no energy left to devote to the ever-increasing speed of the treadmill. With more people stressing the systems the government's net is becoming thinner and thinner with larger holes. Now people are beginning to fall through. Widows, orphans, men and women are beginning to suffer. The solution is a larger, tighter family structure to allow for more resources, and a better, more secure life now and in the twilight years to come. Polygamy in its various forms offers a safety net as well as increased resources needed to live in an increasingly difficult world.

Whether one chooses polyamory, where one husband could take over if the other falls ill or dies, or whether one chooses polyandry, where multiple fathers pool resources for the sake and betterment of the mother and child, or whether one chooses polygyny where multiple women and one man share the work of raising children and running the household, an increasing number of people will entertain alternatives and find better suited forms of marriage according to their situations and personalities.

Polygamy by Country

In countries that do not permit polygamy, the practice is considered bigamy. The word itself indicates the marriage to two women at one time, but has come to mean marriage to two or more wives at once. Such laws usually exist to protect the rights of an unsuspecting second spouse and any children from the otherwise invalid marriage.

Africa

Polygamy existed all over Africa as an aspect of culture or/and religion. Plural marriages have been more common than not in the history of Africa. Many African societies saw children as a form of wealth, thus the more children a family had the more powerful it was. Thus polygamy was part of empire building. It was only during the colonial era that plural marriage was perceived as taboo. Esther Stanford, an African-focused lawyer, states that this decline was encouraged because the issues of property ownership conflicted with European colonial interest. Polygamy is very common in West Africa. However, the diffusion of Islam to this region has counter-intuitively decreased the prevalence of polygamy in this region, due to restrictions on number of wives.

Kenya

Polygamy is widespread in Kenya, the most prominent individual being Akuku Danger who married over 100 wives.

Nigeria

Generally, Nigeria follows the pattern laid out by Islamic Law. After a BBC television interview with Mohammed Bello Abubakar, articles were published in newspapers around the world about his 86 wives and 170 children, and he faced the death penalty under Sharia law if he did not divorce 82 of them.

South Africa

In South Africa, traditionalists commonly practice polygamy. The president, Jacob Zuma follows traditional African tribal culture and is also openly in favor of plural marriages, being married to three wives himself. He has a total of twenty children with these and two previous wives.

Sudan

Sudanese President, Omar Hassan al-Bashir has encouraged multiple marriages to increase the population.

Asia

The Chinese culture of Confucianism permitted polygamy, and thus the practice of polygamy spread from China to Japan and areas that are now Vietnam. Before their modernizations, East Asian countries permitted similar practices of polygamy. The practice is now prohibited.

South Asia

Polygamy, permitted under Islamic law, is present among some Muslims in South Asia.

India

Polygamy is illegal in India for Hindus and other religious groups under the Hindu marriage Act. It remains legal for Muslims under the terms of The Muslim Personal Law (Shariat) Application Act of 1937, as interpreted by the All India Muslim Personal Law Board.

Polygamy is generally quite rare in urban areas, and among the cosmopolitan middle classes because of the cost to maintain multiple wives.

Thailand

Until polygamy was outlawed by King Rama VI, wealthy or upper-class Thai men were historically recognized to maintain mansions consisting of multiple wives and their children in the same residence. Among the royalty and courtiers in the past, wives were classified as principal, secondary, and slave. Today, the tradition of minor wives still remains, but the practice is different from that of the past. Due to the expense involved, minor wives are mostly limited to the wealthy men. While a "proper woman" must remain faithful to her husband, there were no equivalent rules in history mandating fidelity for the man.

Regardless of the historical acceptance, male polygamy or plural marriage is no longer legally or socially acceptable in the contemporary Thai society. However, the practice of having "minor wives" continues in modern days in secrecy from the "primary wife".

Almost all married Thai women today object to this practice, and indeed for many it has been grounds for divorce. Minor wives are viewed with contempt by the Thai society along the same lines of the western idea of a lover or mistress.

China

During the Han Dynasty, it became unlawful for Chinese men to have more than one wife. However, throughout the history of imperial China, it had been common for the rich and influential Chinese men to have one wife and various concubines. Polygamy in China is considered to be a by-product of the tradition of emphasis on procreation and the continuity of the father's family name. Although the establishment of the Republic of China made it unlawful for a man to have multiple spouses. The law outlawed concubines also. Such legislation was generally not enforced, especially among the societal elites who were most likely to live such lifestyles. The most serious changes occurred during and after the Communist Revolution, where the tradition was considered backward and feudal. Polygamy was outlawed and severely punished. It is illegal in modern China to have more than one spouse for either sex. However, polygamy is still seen in southwest China among Chinese minorities such as Tibetans.

Hong Kong

In Hong Kong, polygamy was banned in October 1971. Some Hong Kong businessmen have concubines across the border in mainland China, but concubines do not have the legal or social status of wives and so this should not strictly be called "polygamy". Kevin Murphy of *The International Herald Tribune* reported the cross-border polygamy phenomenon in Hong Kong in 1995.

The traditional attitude toward mistresses is reflected in the saying: "wife is not as good as concubine, concubine is not as good as prostitute, prostitute is not as good as secret affair, secret affair is not as good as the affair you want but can't get".

United States

Although the number of polygamists living in the U.S. is large and growing, for the most part the relationships are not brought about by economic pressures or the societal pressures of a decreased male population. The influences bringing about the institution tend to be religious or the simple fact that men and women have rejected societies idea that there must be one and only one true love in life or way to express a relationship with loved ones.

David Friedman and Steve Sailer have argued that polygamy tends to benefit most women and disadvantage most men, under the assumption that most men and women do not practice it. The idea is that many women would prefer half or one third of someone especially appealing to them instead of being the single spouse of someone that doesn't provide as much economic or utility to them. The remaining women who prefer monogamy will have a better market for finding a spouse themselves. Say that 20% of women are married to 10% of men leaves 90% of men to compete over the remaining 80% of women.

This same result of polygamy is used to justify it as a way to improve the genetic characteristics in a population, the logic being that women will generally tend to marry men of wealth and health. Intelligence has a high correlation with wealth, thus polygamy has the effect of increasing the intelligence inside the population that practices it.

Friedman uses this viewpoint to argue in favor of legalizing polygamy, while Sailer uses it to argue against legalizing it. If polygamy is practiced, as in the middle-east and Imperial China, by only the wealthy and elite and if we agree with the assumption that generally intelligence precedes status and wealth, and if we agree that these men will seek out the highest qualities in females to make their wives, it leaves us with a plain and obvious conclusion that the best genetic qualities will be concentrated in the top 30% of the population, leaving the bottom 70% with an imbalance of desirable qualities.

The idea of a male population of even 10% who are disenfranchised from sex or marriage may destabilize the society, leading to competition, disenfranchisement, and violence, as it did in one of the U.S. polygamous sect of the FLDS, which we will discuss later. With 30% of the population, under this manufactured scenario, being the brightest and most capable that leaves the bottom 70% of the population to produce a less desirable offspring, since the mix of superior genetic traits would not be allowed to enhance the weaker traits.

This may lead to stratification within society. Now we have a more homogenous mix of attributes and genetic traits, leading to an overall balance, in a polygamous society we would have the elite, wealthy and bright representing a ruling oligarchy, and the rest of society in time would become a lesser class.

Although one may easily argue the existence of such a class now, with the elite male wielding power and being able to choose better mates, (and I would not disagree) the scenario brought about by polygamy would speed the process forward. The question is if the scenario of self-imposed eugenics is a good or bad prospect. In the eyes of many, it is not such a bad outcome. It is possible that the number of people choosing polygamy would be small enough it would not impact society at all. This is the conclusion of many leaders.

In the US, the Libertarian Party supports complete decriminalization of polygamy as part of a general belief that the government should not regulate marriages. Feminists and advocates such as Wendy McElroy also support the freedom for adults to voluntarily enter polygamous marriages.

The American Civil Liberties Union of Utah, USA, is opposed to Utah's law against cohabitation.

Looking at the Numbers

We have examined the possible effects of polygamy on gene pools and on the distribution of available females in a polygamous society. The facts were more than borne out in the recent self-destruction of a polygamist sect in the U.S. In this small sect, located in the southwest, men began taking more than one wife.

In true Orwellian style, the more established and politically connected men received their choice of brides. These men were almost invariably older and more politically tied to the leader, either through family lineage, support or money. As the number of available women decreased, the older men begin excommunicating the younger male members in order to do away with competition and their complaints. It did not take long before there was a noticeable lack of able manpower and an overpopulation of unhappy females. As the marriageable women of proper age were taken, the men began to force younger and younger women into marriage. The feeding frenzy ended when pre-pubescent girls were forced to marry middle-aged men in the name of God, religion, and their leader.

The events outlined a microcosmic view, which would occur over time in the macrocosm of general society if there were no limits placed on institutions such as marriage.

Stanley Kurtz, a fellow at the Hudson Institute, defends the traditionally monogamous family structure by standing against the modern arguments increasingly being made by various intellectuals who call for de-criminalizing polygamy. Kurtz concluded, "*Marriage, as its ultramodern critics would like to say, is indeed about choosing one's partner, and about freedom in a society that values freedom. But that's not the only thing it is about. As the Supreme Court justices who unanimously decided Reynolds in 1878 understood, marriage is also about sustaining the conditions in which freedom can thrive. Polygamy in all its forms is a recipe for social structures that inhibit and ultimately undermine social freedom and democracy. A hard-won lesson of Western history is that genuine democratic self-rule begins at the hearth of the monogamous family.*"

Kurtz goes on to say: "*It's getting tougher to laugh off the "slippery slope" argument — the claim that gay marriage will lead to polygamy, polyamory, and ultimately to the replacement of marriage itself by an infinitely flexible partnership system. We've now got a movement for legalized polyamory and the abolition of marriage in Sweden. The Netherlands has given legal, political, and public approval to a cohabitation contract for a polyamorous bisexual triad.*

Two out of four reports on polygamy commissioned by the Canadian government recommended decriminalization and regulation of the practice. And now comes Big Love, HBO's domestic drama about an American polygamous family."

Kurtz goes on to explain that legalizing gay marriage will likely give way to laws allowing for polyamory and polygamy. He stands solidly against the "slippery slope" but not for the reasons one may think. Kurtz addresses the argument that making laws against certain types of unions flies in the face of democracy. The argument states that in a democracy one should have the ability to choose how and in what family structure one lives. Kurtz points to the fact that almost without exception, where there is polygamy there is inequality and lack of democracy.

Kurtz argument may not hold up to scrutiny since the societies he speaks of are driven by the religious rule of Islamic law and not by a simple desire to have freedom of choice. Kurtz seems to believe that allowing polygamy will result in some type of religious takeover. One must keep in mind that religious belief is only one component in an array of reasons people may choose polygamy. However, Kurtz could be correct in his assumption that legalizing gay marriage could open the gates to the freedom of choice regarding polygamy, polyandry, and polyamory, as proven by the movement in Sweden and the Netherlands. It should be pointed out that Sweden and the Netherlands do not seem on their way to becoming oppressive or unjust societies any time soon.

Failure within any institution of marriage, be it monogamous or polygamous, does not speak to the institution itself, but to the failure of people. To believe otherwise would certainly condemn traditional marriage with its 52% failure rate. Monogamy is not dead. It simply does not work for some people. It should be one of several choices offered to the individual. The inability of people to use common sense, balance and self-control would prove equally disastrous for any relationship model. Greed, selfishness and lust can disrupt a traditional marriage as easily as a non-traditional one.

More Data to Consider

Both the Bible and the Koran speak of polygamy in very positive terms as mechanisms by which widows may be supported, loved and protected, and a system in which orphans may be nurtured and raised. Polygamy also balances out and corrects disturbances in populations brought about by war, famine, and catastrophe. Any time a population becomes deprived of males or females, institutions of polygyny and polyandry tend to emerge in order to save the society.

The ratio of women to men vary throughout the world. In the U.S. the surplus of women is a result of men dying in wars, violent crimes, and women outliving men. The upsurge in homosexuality further confuses the issue. Before we count this group into our data we must discern if there is a great difference between the number of gays and lesbian. If there were little difference between the groups the numbers would cancel themselves out. There is another caveat. Female infanticide is still practiced in the world. China and India within their more rural areas have a much higher occurrence than world average of the practice. This has effected the male to female ratios. We have seen the effects of this in recent news. Gang rapes are reported on buses and in the streets of India. Many have gone unpunished. This speaks volumes about what happens when a society is not in balance. In such a radical case it is polyandry that may be the solution.

In 1993, a team at the Harvard School of Public Health reported that 6.2 percent of men and 3.6 percent of women reported a same-sex partner in the previous five years. Marketing consultant Grant Lukenbill reports in his book *Untold Millions* that a 1993 survey of consumer behavior by Yankelovich Partners found that 5 percent of the men contacted identified themselves as gay men, and 6.4 of the women identified themselves as lesbians. A 1993 survey by the Louis Harris organization had results that were confusing, to say the least. They found that 3.8 percent of the men and 2.8 percent of the women had a same-sex partner in the last year; and 4.4 percent of the men and 3.6 percent of the women had a same-sex partner in the last five years; but 1.8 percent of the men and 2.1 percent of the women reported a same-sex partner in the previous month. If we look at the data of all tests and attempt to come to a mean result, given the general allowance for error rate, it should be safe to disregard the gay population in the data since the gay and lesbian groups come close to canceling each other out.

Within the heterosexual world, where women outnumber men, there is a choice forced upon the women who wish to have a relationship or a child. Do they become the "other woman," do they get pregnant and raise a child alone, or do they live without a relationship? In a free society these should not be the only choices.

Bertrand Russell wrote, "And in all countries where there is an excess of women, it is an obvious injustice that those women who, by arithmetical necessity, must remain unmarried should be wholly debarred from sexual experience." Polygamy, then, is a responsible solution for this predicament.

Country	Male Population	Female Population
Russia	46.1%	53.9%
UK	48.6%	51.5%
USA	48.8%	51.2%
Brazil	49.7%	50.27%

There is a growing number of unmarried women, 34 million of them are in the United States. One out of every five women today has no potential mate because there are simply not enough single men to go around. They are alone because of an undersupply of men. Because women tend to outlive men situation for the women become more difficult as they age. Divorce has become a game of musical chairs since divorced men are much more likely than divorced women to remarry. Because it is a buyer's market with the supply of women out stripping demand, men tend to marry younger women. This further exacerbates the problem for older ladies. At this time there are more than twice as many single women as there are single men in their 40s. Women who divorce at 35 are likely to remain single for life and the later in life she divorces the more likely she is to die unattached or with a lover who is legally married to another women. Few people wish to be alone but the modern woman may wish to retain greater autonomy, thus an increasing number of single women are opting for involvement with married men.

Adding to the problem is the number of women who are not financially maintained by a husband. In many cases this means there are more women who have no insurance or health care of any sort. In multiple studies, upon being separated or divorced a financial weight falls much heavier on the wife than the husband. After divorce the finances of the man improves over time, while the financial status of women decreases. This can be a cause of abuse and prostitution in the society as women fall victim to conditions they would not tolerate in other circumstances.

The problem of the unbalanced sex ratios can worsen during times of war. After the WWII there were over 7 million more women than men in Germany. Over 3 million were widowed due to the conflict. There were 100 men aged 20 to 30 for every 167 women in that age group. That is a very large discrepancy of 66% more women than men. Many of these women were exploited.

All of the conditions described above are what the Bible and the Koran endeavored to mitigate by allowing polygamy.

It is said that polygamy allows conformity to human nature. This should be determined on an individual basis. In general men desire sex more frequently than women and men desire more variety. This certainly sounds sexist but generally proves out over a population. Many scientists view this urge as a trait programmed in to better serve the perpetuation of the species as healthy men are chosen by multiple women to receive their traits and raise more robust offspring. Of course, women enjoy variety also and the number of women having affairs speaks to the fact things are not one sided.

New studies show a genetic trait linked to the amount of oxytocin an individual produces. Oxytocin is directly linked to pair-bonding. People with high amounts tend to be more faithful to their mate. This may indicate infidelity is influenced by our genes. The study also revealed less oxytocin in men than women.

Overall, patterns of sexual desire seem to be follow normal difference between the genders, although the degree of difference varies and thus there will be some women that have more desire than men. For those women polyandry may be the answer.

A pregnant women will be incapable of reproduction for up to a year but men can continue to do their part in reproduction. A man is capable of keeping a large number of females pregnant and is so inclined as part of the primitive impulses to keep humanity growing. This is the internal directive of all creatures. Further, women may become infertile by the time they are 45 years of age, with ever increasing genetic errors found in children of women past the age of 36. Some men can continue their reproductive part until overtaken by sickness or death. However, recent studies show that aged men, even with mating with younger women, tend to produce less healthy and less intelligent children than there younger male counterparts. All things have their limits.

All of these traits and conditions are those left us by our primitive ancestors. Many of these urges and conditions tend to run counter to the demands of societies and religions. All this leaves us in a constant state of conflict between our primitive urges and our frontal lobe, as reason battles instinct.

History

Around the world and throughout the ages polygamy has been practiced. Over time, laws formed governing the institution. Some laws protected the first wife against being simply replaced. If this were allowed to occur the benefits of polygamy would be lost, leaving only a man's desire as the guiding force.

Many ancient societies offered protection to wives against a second wife or co-wife. The Babylonian Code of Hammurabi stipulated that in the absence of special circumstances (such as infertility, sickness or misconduct of the first wife), the existing wife first had to agree to the second union. Only among the Greeks and Romans was there any effort by civil authority to enforce monogamy for legitimate marriage. One Greek marriage contract reads, "It shall not be lawful for Philiscus to bring in another wife besides Appolonia."

However, concubinage was universally practiced in all ancient societies as illustrated in the famous quote from Pseudo-Demosthenes (4th century BCE), "Mistresses we keep for the sake of pleasure, concubines for the daily care of our persons, but wives to bear us legitimate children and to be faithful guardians of our households." A concubine was not a legal wife, but a slave woman who lived with a man (often married) to provide regular sexual relations. Children of this type of union were not considered legitimate.

Polygamy was not only common among Jews in ancient times but was practiced in the apostolic era and the age of the church fathers. Josephus, the first-century Jewish historian mentioned that the "ancient practice among us to have many wives at the same time" continued in his day. The church father Justin Martyr (110-165) mentions that in his time Jewish men were permitted to have four or five wives. His comment echoes the attitude of the Jewish Mishnah, codified in writing in the second century CE. Rabbinic scholars assumed the continuance of plural marriage and imposed rules for treatment of multiple wives and their children in estate matters. They even laid down that the maximum number of wives that a man may marry is eighteen based on the example of David, but in general they discouraged taking more than four or five wives for practical reasons. A man should not create a family he cannot support equally.

The famous 12th century Sephardic legal scholar, physician, and philosopher, Moses Maimonides (1135-1204) supported Talmudic tradition and reiterated laws regulating plural marriage in volume four of his Code called, The Book of

Women.

When Israel became a state in 1949, Gershom's ban became legally binding on all Jewish residents. The only accommodation that was made allowed those who came to Israel with more than one wife to keep their family intact, but no new wives could be added. Yet some Sephardic Jews in Israel continued to take second wives in "underground" marriages performed by rabbis who opposed the legal ban.

Polygamy among Jews is not limited to Sephardim. Jews living in Yemen and Ethiopia practice polygamy under the belief that Israel's rabbis are wrong in their prohibition of plural marriage.

Another group of polygamists associating with Judaism are the "Black Hebrews," some 2,000 black Americans who emigrated illegally from urban Chicago to Israel in the early 1970s, claiming to be descendants of one of the (so-called) lost tribes of Israel.

Perhaps the first known Christian leaders to advocate plural marriage were Basilides and Carpocrates, early second century religious teachers in Alexandria, Egypt. They were condemned as heretics by the Church, more for their theology than their marriage beliefs.

Tertullian (160 A.D.) wrote: "each pronouncement and arrangement is (the act) of one and the same God; who did then indeed, in the beginning, send forth a sowing of the race by an indulgent laxity granted to the reins of connubial alliances, until the world should be replenished, until the material of the new discipline should attain to forwardness: now, however, at the extreme boundaries of the times, has checked (the command) which He had sent out, and recalled the indulgence which He had granted."

The arrogance of some of the church fathers has always fascinated me. With polygamy continuing in the time of Jesus and the apostles, and with their acknowledgement of its existence but with no negative comment, save the admonition by Paul to limit marriage to one wife if one wished to serve the church, Tertullian purports to know the mind and intent of God more accurately than God's own son and servants.

In the 3rd century, Eusebius of Caesarea, wrote the lost work "On the Numerous Progeny of the Ancients". This has been given as an example of plural marriage being reconciled with the ascetic life. Since we do not have the book, but only references to it and its contents we do not know what information it contained. It is likely that the problem the book dealt with was the balance presented by the desire of the biblical Patriarchs for numerous offspring and the growing belief that monogamy was the divine template, a stance held church fathers of the time. The problem the theologians faced was that Christianity was considered the spiritual offspring of Judaism, which permitted polygamy.

Augustine wrote *That the good purpose of marriage, however, is better promoted by one husband with one wife, than by a husband with several wives, is shown plainly enough by the very first union of a married pair, which was made by the Divine Being Himself.*

This example does not stand up to scrutiny since at the time of the union of Adam and Eve the world was perfect. They were told to "replenish" the earth, making one wonder how or by whom it was "plenished" in the first place. Only after the fall did procreation begin, along with the struggle of childbirth, and the necessity of acquisition of food and shelter. Polygamy lends itself to a better chance for survival since children are raised to hunt, gather, work the fields, and generally assist in providing for the extended family. Children provide for the parents in the later years their mothers and fathers. Families extend to become tribes and tribes become nations. Each step along the way provides more and more protection and influence in the area. Outside the protection afforded to mankind within the garden, polygamy was a benefit.

Basil of Caesarea (330 – 379 A.D.) wrote; "such a state is no longer called marriage but polygamy or, indeed, a moderate fornication." He ordered that those who are engaged in it should be excommunicated for up to five years, and "only after they have shown some fruitful repentance" were they to be allowed back into the church. Moreover, he stated that that the teachings against plural marriage are "accepted as our usual practice, not from the canons but in conformity with our predecessors." However, the predecessors he spoke of were Romans, not Jews.

Socrates Scholasticus wrote in the 5th century, that the Roman Emperor Valentinian I, in the fourth century, took two wives and authorized his subjects to take two wives supporting the idea that Christians were practicing plural marriage at that time.

 There is no trace of such an edict in any of the extant Roman Laws. Valentinian I divorced his first wife according to John Malalas, the Chronicon Paschale and John of Nikiu, before marrying his mistress, which was viewed as bigamy by Socrates, since the Church did not accept divorce.

A Brief History of Polygamy in Christianity

Before we go down the Christian path of argument each of us must decide if we believe what is in the bible and how we interpret what is written. Presenting a traditional Christian or biblical viewpoint is totally irrelevant if one does not subscribe to that faith or believe the bible is an inspired book to be followed. Moreover, the "traditional" viewpoint is the modern viewpoint and in no way takes into consideration the fact that early Christians and even the Catholic Church allowed polygamy in times when the population contained many more women than men due to death in war.

Christianity began its existence as a sect of Judaism, which allowed polygamy from the time of Lamech. The first instance of polygamy in the Bible was that of Lamech in Genesis 4:19: "Lamech married two women." The names of the women were Adah and Zillah. According to Ussher's Bible chronology, this was about 1000 years after creation, or about 3000 B.C. Several prominent men in the Old Testament were polygamists. Abraham, Jacob, David, Solomon, and others all had multiple wives. Polygamy continued from that day and was accepted into Christianity as Jews converted and continued to marry.

Although polygamy existed in the time of Jesus, he did not

speak against it. Nowhere in the New Testament is the practice condemned or curtailed.

This statement is echoed by Father Eugene Hillman, who has proclaimed, 'Nowhere in the New Testament is there any explicit commandment that marriage should be monogamous or any explicit commandment forbidding polygamy."

As an accepted practice among ancient Jews, polygamy would have been very familiar to the Jewish apostles. It would only be natural for the early congregations, consisting of mostly Jewish members, to include polygamous families. The New Testament does not handle polygamy forthrightly as the Old Testament, but there are a number of allusions or inferences regarding the practice.

When John the Baptist rebukes King Herod for committing adultery, the fact that Herod's father just before that time lived with nine wives receives no censure.

In the parable of the ten virgins (Matt 25:1-13) there is no mention of the bride simply because the virgins are the brides. In fact, copyists of New Testament manuscripts recognized the straightforward meaning and added "and bride" to a number of manuscripts at the end of Matthew 25:1. As mentioned above in the quote from Maimonides, Jewish law permitted marrying multiple wives at the same time and no doubt some Israelite kings built their polygamous households in this manner.

In 1 Corinthians 5:1 Paul rebukes the church for tolerating a man's immoral relations with his father's wife, the same sin committed by Reuben who slept with his father's wife, Bilhah (Gen 35:22). This kind of immorality did not exist among the immoral Gentiles, because incest was banned among the Greeks and Romans.

In 1 Corinthians 6:15-20 Paul likens the relationship of believers to the Lord as a marriage. The allusion Paul is drawing upon is that while the husband is polygamous; the wives are all monogamous to him. Each believer must be faithful to the Lord and not give his body to a harlot.

In 1 Timothy 3:2, 12, Paul restricts a minister to one wife, implying that polygamy was not uncommon among early believers.

Paul's instruction concerning widows (1 Tim 5:14-16) sounds remarkably like application of the Torah obligation for marrying the widow of a brother without a male heir. In 1 Timothy 5:3-16, Paul rules that widows over 60 would be supported by the congregation if there were no family members to assume the duty, but those under 60 were expected to get married (1 Tim 5:14). Paul expresses a strong desire that young widows (those of childbearing age) receive security from their families. It is not unthinkable that in his Jewish understanding he would expect the nearest male relative to take on the Torah responsibility.

Paul adds a requirement not explicitly found in the Torah, but implied. In verse 16 he directs believing women to accept the responsibility of young widows into their family. In other words, the believing wife is to accept the responsibility of her husband complying with the Torah obligation or possibly even taking a needy widow of her own blood relation as a wife to provide for her needs.

To keep all of this in context let us look at 1 Timothy 3 – 5.

1 Timothy 3

New International Version (NIV)

Qualifications for Overseers and Deacons

3 Here is a trustworthy saying: Whoever aspires to be an overseer desires a noble task. 2 Now the overseer is to be above reproach, faithful to his wife, temperate, self-controlled, respectable, hospitable, able to teach, 3 not given to drunkenness, not violent but gentle, not quarrelsome, not a lover of money. 4 He must manage his own family well and see that his children obey him, and he must do so in a manner worthy of full[a] respect. 5 (If anyone does not know how to manage his own family, how can he take care of God's church?) 6 He must not be a recent convert, or he may become conceited and fall under the same judgment as the devil. 7 He must also have a good reputation with outsiders, so that he will not fall into disgrace and into the devil's trap.

8 In the same way, deacons are to be worthy of respect, sincere, not indulging in much wine, and not pursuing dishonest gain. 9 They must keep hold of the deep truths of the faith with a clear conscience. 10 They must first be tested; and then if there is nothing against them, let them serve as deacons.

11 In the same way, the women are to be worthy of respect, not malicious talkers but temperate and trustworthy in everything.

12 A deacon must be faithful to his wife and must manage his children and his household well. 13 Those who have served well gain an excellent standing and great assurance in their faith in Christ Jesus.

Reasons for Paul's Instructions

14 Although I hope to come to you soon, I am writing you these instructions so that, 15 if I am delayed, you will know how people ought to conduct themselves in God's household, which is the church of the living God, the pillar and foundation of the truth. 16 Beyond all question, the mystery from which true godliness springs is great:

He appeared in the flesh,

was vindicated by the Spirit,

was seen by angels,

was preached among the nations,

was believed on in the world,

was taken up in glory.

1 Timothy 4

New International Version (NIV)

4 The Spirit clearly says that in later times some will abandon the faith and follow deceiving spirits and things taught by demons. 2 Such teachings come through hypocritical liars, whose consciences have been seared as with a hot iron. 3 They forbid people to marry and order them to abstain from certain foods, which God created to be received with thanksgiving by those who believe and who know the truth. 4 For everything God created is good, and nothing is to be rejected if it is received with thanksgiving, 5 because it is consecrated by the word of God and prayer.

6 If you point these things out to the brothers and sisters, you will be a good minister of Christ Jesus, nourished on the truths of the faith and of the good teaching that you have followed. 7 Have nothing to do with godless myths and old wives' tales; rather, train yourself to be godly. 8 For physical training is of some value, but godliness has value for all things, holding promise for both the present life and the life to come. 9 This is a trustworthy saying that deserves full acceptance. 10 That is why we labor and strive, because we have put our hope in the living God, who is the Savior of all people, and especially of those who believe.

11 Command and teach these things. 12 Don't let anyone look down on you because you are young, but set an example for the believers in speech, in conduct, in love, in faith and in purity. 13 Until I come, devote yourself to the public reading of Scripture, to preaching and to teaching. 14 Do not neglect your gift, which was given you through prophecy when the body of elders laid their hands on you.

15 Be diligent in these matters; give yourself wholly to them, so that everyone may see your progress. 16 Watch your life and doctrine closely. Persevere in them, because if you do, you will save both yourself and your hearers.

1 Timothy 5

New International Version (NIV)

Widows, Elders and Slaves

5 Do not rebuke an older man harshly, but exhort him as if he were your father. Treat younger men as brothers, 2 older women as mothers, and younger women as sisters, with absolute purity.

3 Give proper recognition to those widows who are really in need. 4 But if a widow has children or grandchildren, these should learn first of all to put their religion into practice by caring for their own family and so repaying their parents and grandparents, for this is pleasing to God. 5 The widow who is really in need and left all alone puts her hope in God and continues night and day to pray and to ask God for help. 6 But the widow who lives for pleasure is dead even while she lives. 7 Give the people these instructions, so that no one may be open to blame. 8 Anyone who does not provide for their relatives, and especially for their own household, has denied the faith and is worse than an unbeliever.

9 No widow may be put on the list of widows unless she is over sixty, has been faithful to her husband, 10 and is well known for her good deeds, such as bringing up children, showing hospitality, washing the feet of the Lord's people, helping those in trouble and devoting herself to all kinds of good deeds.

11 As for younger widows, do not put them on such a list. For when their sensual desires overcome their dedication to Christ, they want to marry. 12 Thus they bring judgment on themselves, because they have broken their first pledge. 13 Besides, they get into the habit of being idle and going about from house to house. And not only do they become idlers, but also busybodies who talk nonsense, saying things they ought not to. 14 So I counsel younger widows to marry, to have children, to manage their homes and to give the enemy no opportunity for slander. 15 Some have in fact already turned away to follow Satan.

16 If any woman who is a believer has widows in her care, she should continue to help them and not let the church be burdened with them, so that the church can help those widows who are really in need.

17 The elders who direct the affairs of the church well are worthy of double honor, especially those whose work is preaching and teaching. 18 For Scripture says, "Do not muzzle an ox while it is treading out the grain, and "The worker deserves his wages." 19 Do not entertain an accusation against an elder unless it is brought by two or three witnesses. 20 But those elders who are sinning you are to reprove before everyone, so that the others may take warning. 21 I charge you, in the sight of God and Christ Jesus and the elect angels, to keep these instructions without partiality, and to do nothing out of favoritism.

22 Do not be hasty in the laying on of hands, and do not share in the sins of others. Keep yourself pure.

23 Stop drinking only water, and use a little wine because of your stomach and your frequent illnesses.

24 The sins of some are obvious, reaching the place of judgment ahead of them; the sins of others trail behind them. 25 In the same way, good deeds are obvious, and even those that are not obvious cannot remain hidden forever.

The Roman emperor, Valentinian I, in the fourth century, authorized Christians to take two wives. In the eighth century Charlemagne, holding power over both church and state, practiced polygamy, having six wives.

St. Augustine, one of the most influential church fathers, declared that polygamy was not a crime where it was the legal institution of a country. He wrote in *The Good of Marriage* (chapter 15, paragraph 17), that polygamy "was lawful among the ancient fathers: whether it be lawful now also, I would not hastily pronounce. For there is not now necessity of begetting children, as there then was, when, even when wives bear children, it was allowed, in order to get a more numerous posterity, to marry other wives in addition, which now is certainly not lawful."

He declined to judge the patriarchs, but did not deduce from their practice the ongoing acceptability of polygamy. In another place, he wrote, "Now indeed in our time, and in keeping with Roman custom, it is no longer allowed to take another wife, so as to have more than one wife living."

The Church in Rome banned polygamy in order to conform to Greco-Roman culture that prescribed only one legal wife although the church tolerated concubinage and prostitution, which was practiced by a number of Popes and priests outside the command of celibacy for the clergy.

During the Protestant Reformation, Martin Luther said, "I confess for my part that if a man wishes to marry two or more wives, I cannot forbid him for it does not contradict the Scripture." He advised Philip of Hesse that he should keep his second marriage a secret to avoid public scandal.

Other Christian advocates of polygamy arose in the 17th and 18th centuries, most notably John Milton (1608-1674), the famous author of Paradise Lost, Martin Madan (1726-1790), an itinerant English preacher in the Calvinist Methodist movement and author of Thelyphthora, or A Treatise on Female Ruin, and Wesley Hall (1711-1776), brother-in-law to John Wesley and dedicated evangelist. Hall had the distinction of actually practicing polygamy and yet many churches and Christian evangelicals supported him throughout his ministry.

Many modern Christians may find it difficult to believe but there are Christ-centered, Bible-believing conservative Christians espousing and living in plural marriages. Polygamy as a cultural phenomenon among Protestant Christians came into existence (or came out of the closet) in the early 1990s and should not be confused with Mormon polygamy. The theological and Scriptural foundations are totally different for the two systems. Protestant polygamists, while espousing traditional Christian doctrines, believe strongly that Scripture permits polygamy and the church should recognize that fact. The following is a review of what the Bible says about polygamy.

In the beginning God commanded Adam and Eve to multiply their descendants and fill the earth (Gen 1:22; 9:1). Thus, marriage has been God's normative pattern and will for men and women since Creation. He wants every man to be married and every woman to have a husband (cf. Gen 2:18, 21-24; 1 Cor 7:2; 11:7-9). For descendants to multiply, marriages multiplied and at some point men decided it would be good to have multiple wives. With the revelation of the Torah to Israel God demonstrated His acceptance of polygamy. The Lord's legislation was not designed to regulate polygamy out of existence, but to assure proper treatment for the women and children involved.

One of the greatest poets of the English language and the famous English Puritan, John Milton (1608 - 1674), wrote, 'I have not said 'the marriage of one man with one woman' lest I should by implication charge the holy patriarchs and pillars of our faith, Abraham and others who had more than one wife, at the same time, with habitual sin; and lest I should be forced to exclude from the sanctuary of God as spurious, the whole offspring which sprang from them, yea, the whole of the sons of Israel, for whom the sanctuary itself was made. For it is said in Deuteronomy (xxii. 2,) "A bastard shall not enter into the congregation of Jehovah even to the tenth generation."

In following with the obvious reasons for polygamy laid down before, some of which were to alleviate an imbalance in the population due to war or catastrophe, on February 14, 1650, the parliament at Nürnberg decreed that because so many men were killed during the Thirty Years' War, that every man was allowed to marry up to ten women. This dispensation was kept in place for a time as the population of males increased through birth.

African churches have long recognized polygamy. They stated in the 1988 Lambeth Conference, "It has long been recognized in the Anglican Communion that polygamy in parts of Africa, and traditional marriage, do genuinely have features of both faithfulness and righteousness."

Mwai Kibaki, the Christian president of Kenya, whose victory was attributed to 'the hand of the Lord' by the Presbyterian Church of East Africa, is polygamous. South Africa has recently legalized polygamy, owing in part to the re-establishment of African traditions, which began after the period of apartheid started by the Afrikaner National Party from the 1960s until February 1991. The President of South Africa is a polygamist.

Reformation Period

After the invention of the printing press around 1440, and the publishing of the Bible, a new age of thought and discussion arose and the Renaissance was born. The new era of reason (1400s to 1700s) affected everything from art to religion. At the end of the fifteenth century and the beginning of the sixteenth, Christian humanists sought to apply the new style of reasoning and scholarship to the study of scriptures. The first order of business was to rid the scriptures of the linguistic miss-handling and miss-interpretation by the church. Scriptures were translated from their original languages. The aim and goal was to re-examine each line, word and phrase and thus to return to the true and original meaning of their religion.

In the interests of spreading religious understanding, they began to translate the Bible into the common languages. With greater personal understanding a spiritual revival began. The Renaissance belief in the ability of man to improve himself and his environment made people less content with their condition. The church was corrupt and everyone knew it. The need to reform the church was obvious. It was in possession of vast wealth, and it was exercising great political power over nations and individuals. The papacy granted patronage positions to those that had more interest in lining their pockets than in promoting the welfare of their "flocks". The Christian humanists condemned these people and the church responsible for the graft. A new clergy of men such as Martin Luther were striving for a purer and more authentic church.

The church made it very plain it was stubbornly entrenched. At the Council of Trent in 1563 the Catholic Church voiced its strong opposition to plural marriage. In Canon II of the Doctrine on the Sacrament of Matrimony, the Church declared: "If any one saith, that it is lawful for Christians to have several wives at the same time, and that this is not prohibited by any divine law; let him be anathema." So much for knowing ones bible. In the Decree on the Reformation of Marriage the Church banned "concubinage" in all their lands and called upon the civil authority to enforce this ruling by the most severe punishments to those who did not put away their concubines.

The edict institutionalized monogamy, requiring all weddings to be performed by a priest. The church changed marriage from a personal choice to a lifetime sentence by adopting a stance that marriage was both a sacrament and indissoluble forever.

However, in spite of declaring marriage a sacrament, celibacy became even more sacred. Canon X of the Doctrine on the Sacrament of Matrimony declares: "If any one saith, that the marriage state is to be placed above the state of virginity, or of celibacy, and that it is not better and more blessed to remain in virginity, or in celibacy, than to be united in matrimony; let him be anathema."

Celibacy was ordered by the Church, creating its own version of polygamy by demanding that large numbers of women to disobey the creation mandate, making them unavailable as wives and mothers.

According to the Franciscan Sisters website, "A sister or nun … is a bride of Christ, because He has chosen her for this purpose. Her main identity is as a spouse of Christ. The Lord asks her to sacrifice marriage and family life and to belong to Him alone." Some orders of nuns wear wedding rings to signify their status as wives of Christ. The practice of celibacy imposed on the nuns produced a metaphorical polygamous family with Christ as the husband and thousands of nuns as his wives.

Concubinage may have been outlawed but men routinely had mistresses in Catholic Europe, including the priests, with little or no punishment for the blatant immorality. The Protestant Reformation did little to change the marriage theology or the mating practices of men, thereby fostering wholesale injustice to women. Divorce did not become widely legal until the 19th century, but it was no remedy to the root problem created by the Church. Combined with the Western romantic myth of a right mate for every person, churches have often treated divorced persons as pariahs. If Catholic doctrine were true then with the number of divorces and remarriages in the last century the Body of Christ is in a polygamous mess.

In the 16th century, there was a Christian re-examination of plural marriages. The founder of the Protestant Reformation, Martin Luther wrote: "I confess that I cannot forbid a person to marry several wives, for it does not contradict the Scripture. If a man wishes to marry more than one wife he should be asked whether he is satisfied in his conscience that he may do so in accordance with the word of God. In such a case the civil authority has nothing to do in the matter."

The theologian Philipp Melanchthon counseled that Henry VIII need not risk schism by dissolving his union with the established churches to grant himself divorces in order to replace his barren wives, but could instead look to polygamy as a suitable alternative.

Anabaptist leader, Bernhard Rothmann, initially opposed the idea of plural marriage. However, he later wrote a theological defense of plural marriage, and took 9 wives himself, saying "God has restored the true practice of holy matrimony amongst us."

The Lutheran pastor, Johann Lyser, strongly defended plural marriage in a work entitled "Polygamia Triumphatrix". As a result, he was imprisoned, beaten and exiled from Italy to Holland.

Building on the ideas articulated during the renaissance, Martin Madan produced one of the more notable works regarding the modern concept of Christian Plural Marriage in the 18th century entitled "Thelyphthora". This particular volume set the foundation of what is considered the modern Christian Plural Marriage movement.

Coming Into The Present

John Colenso was the Anglican bishop of Natal, South Africa, in 1853. He was the first to write down the Zulu language. He championed the Zulu way of life, which included plural marriage. Later Colenso's vision would come to fruition when 67-year-old South African president Jacob Zuma married his fourth wife.

In 1869 by James Campbell (pseudonym) published a work entitled "The History and Philosophy of Marriage (or Polygamy and Monogamy Compared)", which aided in explaining the biblical and social thought behind the modern movement of Christian Plural Marriage.

The Nigerian Celestial Church of Christ allows clergy and laymen to keep multiple wives, and the Lutheran Church of Liberia began allowing plural marriage in the 1970s.

Several other denominations permit those already in polygamous marriages to convert and join their church, without having to renounce their multiple marriages. These include the African Instituted Harrist Church, started in 1913.

In the 1988 Lambeth Conference of The Anglican church the

decision was made to admit those who were polygamists at the time they converted to Christianity, subject to certain restrictions. The Anglican Church had been wrestling with the issue since the Lambeth Conference of 1888 where it stated:

"That it is the opinion of this Conference that persons living in polygamy be not admitted to baptism, but they may be accepted as candidates and kept under Christian instruction until such time as they shall be in a position to accept the law of Christ. That the wives of polygamists may, in the opinion of this Conference, be admitted in some cases to baptism, but that it must be left to the local authorities of the Church to decide under what circumstances they may be baptized." (Resolution 5).

A resolution dated 1958 and numbered 120 states that:
"(a) The Conference bears witness to the truth that monogamy is the divine will, testified by the teaching of Christ himself, and therefore true for every race of men,"
but adds:
"(d) The Conference, recognizing that the problem of polygamy is bound up with the limitations of opportunities for women in society, urges that the Church should make every effort to advance the status of women in every possible way, especially in the sphere of education."

In 1988, Resolution 26 declared:

"This Conference upholds monogamy as God's plan, and as the ideal relationship of love between husband and wife; nevertheless recommends that a polygamist who responds to the Gospel and wishes to join the Anglican Church may be baptized and confirmed with his believing wives and children on the following conditions:(1) that the polygamist shall promise not to marry again as long as any of his wives at the time of his conversion are alive;(2) that the receiving of such a polygamist has the consent of the local Anglican community;(3) that such a polygamist shall not be compelled to put away any of his wives, on account of the social deprivation they would suffer;(4) and recommends that provinces where the Churches face problems of polygamy are encouraged to share information of their pastoral approach to Christians who become polygamists so that the most appropriate way of disciplining and pastoring them can be found, and that the ACC be requested to facilitate the sharing of that information."

In 2008, the 114. Resolution of the Lambeth Conference said this:

"In the case of polygamy, there is a universal standard – it is understood to be a sin, therefore polygamists are not admitted to positions of leadership including Holy Orders, nor after acceptance of the Gospel can a convert take another wife, nor, in some areas, are they admitted to Holy Communion."

There are some modern Biblical scholars such as Blaine Robinson who believe that the Bible advocates polygamy. William Luck states that polygamy is not prohibited by the Bible and that it would have been required (as a secondary effect) of a married man who seduced (Ex. 22) or raped (Deut. 22) a virgin, where her father did not veto a marriage.

Here are some Bible verses that report on Polygamy:

Genesis 4:19
And Lamech took unto him two wives.

Genesis 16:1-4
Now Sarai Abram's wife bare him no children: and she had an handmaid, an Egyptian, whose name was Hagar. And Sarai said unto Abram, Behold now, the LORD hath restrained me from bearing: I pray thee, go in unto my maid; it may be that I may obtain children by her. And Abram hearkened to the voice of Sarai. And Sarai ... gave her to her husband Abram to be his wife. And he went in unto Hagar, and she conceived.

Genesis 25:6
But unto the sons of the concubines, which Abraham had....

Genesis 26:34

Esau ... took to wife Judith the daughter of Beeri the Hittite, and Bashemath the daughter of Elon the Hittite.

Genesis 31:17
Then Jacob rose up, and set ... his wives upon camels.

Exodus 21:10
If he take him another wife....

Deuteronomy 21:15
If a man have two wives, one beloved, and another hated....

Judges 8:30
And Gideon had threescore and ten sons of his body begotten: for he had many wives.

1 Samuel 1:1-2
Elkanah ... had two wives; the name of the one was Hannah, and the name of the other Peninnah.

2 Samuel 12:7-8
Thus saith the LORD God of Israel ... I gave thee ... thy master's wives....

1 Kings 11:2-3

Solomon ... had seven hundred wives ... and three hundred concubines.

1 Chronicles 4:5
And Ashur the father of Tekoa had two wives, Helah and Naarah.

2 Chronicles 11:21
Rehoboam ... took eighteen wives, and threescore concubines.

2 Chronicles 13:21
But Abijah waxed mighty, and married fourteen wives....

2 Chronicles 24:3
Jehoiada took for him two wives....

Mt.25:1
Then shall the kingdom of heaven be likened unto ten virgins, which took their lamps, and went forth to meet the bridegroom.

1 Timothy: 2,3 A bishop then must be blameless, the husband of one wife, vigilant, sober, of good behavior, given to hospitality, apt to teach" (Also see verse 12 *"deacons shall have only one wife"*).
These verses in 1 Timothy limit men who could be polygamists to monogamy so they may have more resources left to serve the

church. Since death via martyrdom was likely it was suggested that the Christians not marry at all. Men were allowed to have one wife so he would be less tempted to commit adultery. Fewer wives and children would be left behind if he were monogamous than if he had two or more wives.

Polygamy – A Social Choice

One of the most difficult distinctions to make is the one between social and religious pressures. This became quiet apparent during a trip to Argentina. The plan was to go in with a team and build a church for a certain Pentecostal denomination. I had listened to church teaching and dogma for a couple of years. Some things seemed reasonable. Many did not, but at least the rules were applied across the board with equal rigidity to all. At least that is what I assumed before the aircraft landed.

After driving to the outskirts of Buenos Aires and into the countryside we arrived at the church. Services were being held in a large tent. There we met the church leaders.

In the U.S. version of the church, we were taught that no divorced person could hold a high church office. Certainly no remarried person could ascend to the throne of the pulpit. Now we were building a church so that a large congregation and several pastors, who did not adhere to these rules, could hold services in a brick building. Upon getting to know the pastors it became obvious that they were working under a different set of rules from their North American counterparts. Most of the congregation and all of the pastors were married but none were living with their wives. All were living with a mistress. Most had been with their paramour many years and had children within the second relationship.

For more than a half century Argentina had been under control of very conservative Catholic leaders. Many rules of the church had become law. Divorce was illegal in Argentina at that time. Social pressures had compelled the people to marry young and have children. If the couples separated they had no recourse but to continue their lives alone or in adultery. By adultery, I mean the men were living with a person to whom they were committed but not married.

The circumstances the Catholic church inflicted on the people stifled free will and the natural flow of marriage. Divorce was made illegal. If the Assembly Of God church held to their stated doctrine, forbidding divorced, remarried men or those living in adultery from holding office the church we were building would have few people to manage and expand the denominations in that country. So, does the church stand firm on its convictions or look the other way? In the end, denominations are organizations built on money and numbers. If you are in the U.S. and are a divorced person who is being discriminated against by a church, you should know that if you were the same person in the same denomination in another country you would be treated differently. The view is driven by social conventions.

The other side of the coin is equally amusing. During a trip to Trinidad – Tobago I was teaching a class in religious studies. Afterward a student approached to ask a few questions. He enquired into my church membership and education. When I mentioned the word "Baptist" he recoiled as if being shot.

Later I spoke to our host about the reaction. What I was told made me chuckle, but also heightened my concern about interactions between churches and cultures.

The Spiritual Baptist faith is based in Trinidad and Tobago. It has African influences but Spiritual Baptists consider themselves to be Christians. The Baptist faith was brought to Trinidad by the Merikins, former American slaves who were recruited by the British to fight for them during the Revolutionary War of 1812. Ex-slaves had settled in remote areas of Trinidad.

Whereas Voodoo is in Haiti and is a mixture of Catholicism and African pagan religions, in Trinidad and Tobago, the Spiritual Baptist faith is a mixture of Christian Protestantism and African Paganism and, even though they consider themselves to be Christian, they are related to Voodoo.

What does this have to do with polygamy? Hopefully, these little anecdotes will help us remember that when it comes to what is considered normal, we are dealing with two influences, which can be difficult to separate. The rules of society and those of religion collide and combine. If we wish to have a theological or religious debate we must seek to rightly divide the entangled cords of religion and culture.

In religious communities where there are practices that go contrary to social norms the communities tend to be closed and self-protective. The more their practices deviate from those of the societies in which they are situated the more likely the religious community will evolve into a self-sustaining, self-protective and isolated cult. At the point members begin to dress alike, wear their hair the same, and follow strict codes of conduct as interpreted, dictated, or enforced by a single individual or small unchecked group, they have devolved into a cult. It is in this environment polygamy becomes a dangerous practice because the individual members become subjects and servants of the leaders. Personal choice is eclipsed by the limited, radical thought of one man or group. It is in this environment that arranged marriages and child weddings take place.

If everyone looks and acts alike it is an army or a cult, not a choice. Where personal choice is denied, personal happiness is also denied.

This adage swings both ways. If polygamy is the institution the individuals have chosen and is the foundation of their happiness the denial of polygamy is the destruction of their happiness.

While visiting India, missionaries met a man who had two wives. He had married a woman whom he loved and cared for. She was from a family of four and had a younger sister. Her parents died, leaving her younger sister to live on the streets. The young woman would have been reduced to being a prostitute in order to survive. The older sister approached her husband, asking him if he would love and care for her younger sister, marry her, and save her from the nightmare awaiting her on the streets of Deli. The husband agreed and took the younger sister as his second wife. The two sisters lived in harmony and safety for years, until the missionaries arrived.

After they managed to convert the husband the missionaries informed him it would be necessary to divorce one of his wives or go to hell for adultery. Thus, the Christian preachers assigned a helpless, loving, and innocent young woman to a life of hell as a street prostitute. She was found dead, having been raped, beaten, and stabbed.

The story is true and illustrates the damage and pain unlearned and narrow religious minds can produce. What sense could it possibly make to demand the divorce and destruction of a loving family in exchange for a particular brand of Christianity? Polygamy is not a theological problem. It is a cultural one. Some Eastern cultures permit this state of marriage today. Most Western cultures do not openly embrace polygamy, however, there are several churches practicing it and many groups or subcultures live in households where polygamy is practiced between consenting adults. Church members protect themselves from prosecution by taking one wife as a legal spouse and the other women as spiritual wives, joined by a pastor but not in a civil union.

America has a long history of polygamy beginning with the Indian tribes, all of whom were polygamous when America was colonized. By the mid-1800s each tribal council had banned polygamy to curry favor with the white government and under the influence of white missionaries. Polygamy still persisted among Indians, however, as evidenced by the 1901 census of Oklahoma that asked whether individuals in the household were living in polygamy.

In mainstream America, we have our own issues. Many churches, such as the Church of Christ and other denominations will not allow any person to hold office if they have been remarried. However, in my little area of the conservative South, the majority of members have lived with someone before wedding another. The vast majority had intercourse at least once before getting married to some other person.

The wake-up call is that in Bible times there was no certain or distinct ceremony that marked the official beginning of a marriage. Pagans had various rites, and Jews had theirs, but the actual marriage was marked with sexual intercourse. If you had sex with someone, you were married. Even today marriages may be annulled if intercourse has not taken place. Further, in the Catholic faith there are times when a marriage may be annulled if children are not born and certainly may be annulled if consummation has not taken place.

In following strict rules, especially religious rules we can easily overlook mountains of "sins" and transgressions of one person while excluding and embarrassing good people who have done little if anything wrong.

As an example I will take recent events in the rural county in which I live. One pastor, we will call Tom had a conversion experience when he was 50 years old. Before his conversion Tom was quite the rounder. He loved drinking and having sex with strangers. After his conversion Tom decided to become a pastor. The church celebrated his salvation, conversion, and decision. Tom was called to pastor a small local church.

Larry was a good man and followed the rules all of his life. He grew up in the Baptist church, married and raised two children. Larry's wife began having an affair, quickly leading her to leave the church and divorce Larry. Larry was removed from his position as pastor because the church felt if he could not control his family he could not manage the church. Later, after adjusting to his situation Larry meet and fell in love with a lovely woman. They married. That very month the Baptist church rescinded his ordination and declared he could not be a pastor because he was no longer following their interpretation of being the "husband of one wife".

So we allow the man who had sex with a dozen women, but did not marry until he was fifty, to lead the church because he has been married only once by cultural standards, but we rip a pastor out of the pulpit because his wife left him and he chooses not to die alone. Brilliant!

Judaism and Christianity are Eastern religions. Both were born in the Middle East. We in the west have managed to paint Jesus as a blue-eyed, brown-haired, thin man, when it is far more likely Jesus was a short, stocky, black-haired, brown-eyed individual living happily and without qualm in an area where polygamy was practiced. Even Jesus' archenemy, Herod had two wives, yet within their meeting, when Jesus could have pointed out his flaws, polygamy was not spoken of.

We placed our cultural imprint on how Jesus looked. We have done the same with marriage, stripping away what the Bible says and replacing it with our own societal norms. This is not the greater sin. The real error is to read and interpret the scriptures in this prejudiced light and then to force the error on all others under our authority.

The fastest growing area of polygamy is in the secular population. Detached and apart from the religious communities, the secular community represents a personal and social choice to throw off what some may see as arbitrary rules of society and embrace the choice of living with those one loves. It is not easy, but it represents the decision to live according to one's own heart, even though it is more difficult at times than following the crowd.

Compartments of the Heart

Of all the highest and most insurmountable obstacles to a successful "poly" relationship is the same trip-wire that causes destruction in monogamous relationships, but multiplied. It is the inability to recognize,understand, or admit that men and women think differently. Their brains are not wired, nor do they function the same. Although they are worn out clichés they have a basis in truth; men compartmentalize, don't tend to remember details, and tend to be emotionally more reserved. Women tend to have better memories. They tend to be more emotionally open. They tend to have a more interrelated view of things.

In a polygamous relationship, because of the way men tend to compartmentalize, their emotional connection with one person, women, or spouse will not effect the way the man will feel about the other women or spouses in his life.

Mark B. Kastleman is the author of the revolutionary new book titled The Drug of the New Millennium-the Science of How Internet Pornography Radically Alters the Human Brain and Body-A Guide for Parents, Spouses, Clergy and Counselors.

In a recent article Kastleman writes:

"Significant differences exist between the male and female brains. Although what follows has been meticulously gathered from the research and writings of leading scientists and psychologists, it is by no means a hard and fast rule or description of every man and every woman. Every person is different and unique.

However, the facts clearly bear out that for nearly all men and women there are significant differences between the male and female brain. This means that in most cases, men and women do not behave, feel, think, or respond in the same ways, either on the inside or on the outside.

The male brain is highly specialized, using specific parts of one hemisphere or the other to accomplish specific tasks. The female brain is more diffused and utilizes significant portions of both hemispheres for a variety of tasks.

111

Men are able to focus on narrow issues and block out unrelated information and distractions. Women naturally see everyday things from a broader, "big-picture" vantage point.

Men can narrowly focus their brains on specific tasks or activities for long periods of time without tiring. Women are better equipped to divide their attention among multiple activities or tasks.

Men are able to separate information, stimulus, emotions, relationships, etc. into separate compartments in their brains, while women tend to link everything together.

Men see individual issues with parts of their brain, while women look at the holistic or multiple issues with their whole brain (both hemispheres).

Men have as much as 20 times more testosterone in their systems than do women. This makes men typically more aggressive, dominant and more narrowly focused on the physical aspects of sex.

In men, the dominant perceptual sense is vision, which is typically not the case with women. All of a woman's senses are, in some respects, more finely tuned than those of a man."

Christiane Northrup, M.D., author of Women's Bodies, Women's Wisdom and The Wisdom of Menopause

Adds her opinion by stating:

"Men do this with ease. A little cubby here for work, one for sports, one for being a Daddy and one for being a Husband. His life seems so easily sorted into little sections."

Some researchers say it is in the male genetic code, some say it is learned behavior. Not all men do it, but most have the technique down pat.

While researching this post I quizzed my husband. I wanted to pick his brain on the topic. His response was simple, "We don't compartmentalize, Honey. We organize!"

"It's important to understand that communication challenges in male-female relationships stem from the different ways in which men's and women's brains are wired. "Men compartmentalize their feelings, but women remember everything. So when women bring up issues in a relationship, they tend to bring up everything that is related," she adds, noting that this is a big mistake. That's because most men find this approach overwhelming, or view "hashing over everything" as a character attack."

Likewise, women tend to talk a problem out or through. They are reasoning and examining as they talk, whereas men tend to mull things over and try to come to an answer before speaking. This is one reason why men think women "talk a problem to death," and women comment that "men don't share their feelings and you never know what they are thinking."

One of the problems between sexes is the way they differ in handling emotional damage. In a relationship there will be damage. Being continually reminded of it and dwelling on it is not the answer, but neither is complete compartmentalization, or silence.

Men tend to handle emotional damage like they are a ship at sea. Think of a ship. In large ships there are compartments, which are able to be sealed off in case of damage where water is taken on. It is safer to seal off the damaged compartment and lock it in securely than to go in for repairs. That is the way many men think. This approach does not allow for easy repair of the relationship.

Even if ,through his own words or deeds the relationship is damaged, a man will evaluate the price of repair and decide if the relationship is likely to sink, float, or cost too much in emotional recompense. If the woman is hurt and needs to talk things through the man may view this as an attempt to breach the sealed emotional compartment and react in fear of the pain hidden behind the wall.

Women do not tend to compartmentalize. Their thought process will evaluate the emotional drive to be with their husband and if they want to continue the relationship they will set about attempting to understand and repair it. This, of course, will take communication. She will look at dealing with all parts of the situation all of the time, whereas a man will evaluate dealing with each situation in a succession of segments, if he is comfortable talking about his feelings at all.

The difference allows the woman a more panoramic view and understanding of the entire situation while, for his part, the man is afforded more of an ability to focus totally on the problem or the situation at hand.

It is a wonder that the human race has continued this long, but our strength is in the teamwork and complement between the sexes. Together it is easier to solve problems and conquer our environment. We simply have problems understanding one another enough to work through our differences. Now, multiply that by the number of people in the poly relationship and understand the gravity of the necessity for a game plan of how to argue and disagree with grace and honesty.

How to Choose a Wife (or Husband)

Finding women who are open to polygamy will not be a problem within a small closed polygamist community which is religiously based, such as the FLDS communities. Each community has its own rituals and routines, some arranging marriages between men and brides and some allowing courtships. Within these communities it is obvious as to what the plans and expectations are within the marriage and how one will live when married. Men and women have been conditioned their entire life to accept polygamy as a valid and preferred state of matrimony. Finding someone who wishes to be in a polygamist marriage is obviously not difficult.

Within the religious communities such as these it is not always the men who choose the brides. Marriages may be arranged or men pursue women who are already conditioned and willing to enter in to a family with multiple wives. In the less confined religious communities of the FLDS church, as well as others similar to them, there are other communities such as the Jewish community of old in which the first wife must give consent in order for the husband to marry a second wife. As one could expect a polygamist marriage in these environments are less numerous.

In such cases it may be the wife who selects the next sister wife. Indeed for polygamy to work well the wives must have a say so in who the wives will be. The new wife must be open to polygamy, not jealous or competitive, able and willing to fit in with the existing wives, and the husband must love her and treat her equally. Just as important, the existing wives must love her also. The family must remain a loving and cohesive unit as much without jealousy and division as human nature will allow.

In an open, secular setting, finding and connecting with a person who is open to polygamy is difficult, but it is becoming less so. There are growing numbers of men and women walking away from fundamental religious communities yet still holding on to the belief that polygamy is a viable option and wishing to continue within that state of marriage. There are growing numbers of websites serving as networks and connection points which allow these religious wayfarers, as well as secular polygamists to make contact. A word of warning regarding some websites is in order. Beware. Many sites serve only to seek out willing ladies for the webmaster and a few friends. These sites are a dangerous scam. Men seeking out willing wives may set up a website which looks like an open and free exchange between all who are interested, but the site may simply be a very small group of males trolling for women.

Situations that seem most successful and fool-proof come about when the wife or wives approach a female whom they believe will fit in to the lifestyle and recruit her as the next wife. In this situation the wives have already agreed to the relationship and the possibility of another wife. It is up to the husband then to decide if he can and will love and provide for her. We see this happen often when a wife has a sister or a friend who has experienced difficulty in life, death of a husband, or is in need of being cared for and loved. Stripping away the jealousy that is pervasive to the human species and tapping into pure compassion, one woman loving and caring for another's wellbeing may wish to share her happiness and stability with another. This circumstance seems to work out better than most.

 The husband would be the key to squelching jealousy between the wives and probably the children as well. It would take a truly dedicated and humble husband to do this. He must treat each wife with equal love, claiming them as his own even in the midst of society's scorn. They must feel like they are truly "his." There is a feeling of an emotional and spiritual "covering" like a warm blanket that will descend on the wife who has a safe and loving place.

In Polyandry jealousy tends to be more of an issue. Men seem to be more predisposed to being territorial and thus less willing to share. If males could also strip away the jealousy that is pervasive and if men could tap into pure compassion, man-to-man, instead of competition, polyandry could be implemented and possibly become as commonplace as polygamy.

The God of Polygamy

That God Himself has more than one wife, in a symbol or type, comes as a shock to most Bible believing western Christians. In Ezekiel 23 the Lord speaks of the divided kingdom of Israel as two wives who had committed adultery.

Ezekiel 23 (NIV)

Two Adulterous Sisters

1 The word of the LORD came to me: 2 "Son of man, there were two women, daughters of the same mother. 3 They became prostitutes in Egypt, engaging in prostitution from their youth. In that land their breasts were fondled and their virgin bosoms caressed. 4 The older was named Oholah, and her sister was Oholibah. They were mine and gave birth to sons and daughters. Oholah is Samaria, and Oholibah is Jerusalem.

5 "Oholah engaged in prostitution while she was still mine; and she lusted after her lovers, the Assyrians-warriors 6 clothed in blue, governors and commanders, all of them handsome young men, and mounted horsemen. 7 She gave herself as a prostitute to all the elite of the Assyrians and defiled herself with all the idols of everyone she lusted after. 8 She did not give up the prostitution she began in Egypt, when during her youth men slept with her, caressed her virgin bosom and poured out their lust upon her."

9 *"Therefore I handed her over to her lovers, the Assyrians, for whom she lusted. 10 They stripped her naked, took away her sons and daughters and killed her with the sword. She became a byword among women, and punishment was inflicted on her.*

11 *"Her sister Oholibah saw this, yet in her lust and prostitution she was more depraved than her sister. 12 She too lusted after the Assyrians – governors and commanders, warriors in full dress, mounted horsemen, all handsome young men. 13 I saw that she too defiled herself; both of them went the same way." 14 "But she carried her prostitution still further. She saw men portrayed on a wall, figures of Chaldeans portrayed in red, 15 with belts around their waists and flowing turbans on their heads; all of them looked like Babylonian chariot officers, natives of Chaldea. 16 As soon as she saw them, she lusted after them and sent messengers to them in Chaldea. 17 Then the Babylonians came to her, to the bed of love, and in their lust they defiled her. After she had been defiled by them, she turned away from them in disgust. 18 When she carried on her prostitution openly and exposed her nakedness, I turned away from her in disgust, just as I had turned away from her sister. 19 Yet she became more and more promiscuous as she recalled the days of her youth, when she was a prostitute in Egypt. 20 There she lusted after her lovers, whose genitals were like those of donkeys and whose emission was like that of horses. 21 So you longed for the lewdness of your youth, when in Egypt your bosom was caressed and your young breasts fondled. 22 "Therefore, Oholibah, this is what the Sovereign LORD says: I will*

stir up your lovers against you, those you turned away from in disgust, and I will bring them against you from every side- 23 the Babylonians and all the Chaldeans, the men of Pekod and Shoa and Koa, and all the Assyrians with them, handsome young men, all of them governors and commanders, chariot officers and men of high rank, all mounted on horses. 24 They will come against you with weapons, chariots and wagons and with a throng of people; they will take up positions against you on every side with large and small shields and with helmets. I will turn you over to them for punishment, and they will punish you according to their standards. 25 I will direct my jealous anger against you, and they will deal with you in fury. They will cut off your noses and your ears, and those of you who are left will fall by the sword. They will take away your sons and daughters, and those of you who are left will be consumed by fire. 26 They will also strip you of your clothes and take your fine jewelry. 27 So I will put a stop to the lewdness and prostitution you began in Egypt. You will not look on these things with longing or remember Egypt anymore.

28 "For this is what the Sovereign LORD says: I am about to hand you over to those you hate, to those you turned away from in disgust. 29 They will deal with you in hatred and take away everything you have worked for. They will leave you naked and bare, and the shame of your prostitution will be exposed. Your lewdness and promiscuity 30 have brought this upon you, because you lusted after the nations and defiled yourself with their idols. 31 You have gone the way of your sister; so I will put her cup into your hand. 32 "This is what the Sovereign LORD says: "You will drink your sister's cup, a cup large and deep; it will bring scorn and derision, for it holds so much. 33 You will be filled with drunkenness and sorrow, the cup of ruin and desolation, the cup of your sister Samaria.

34 You will drink it and drain it dry; you will dash it to pieces and tear your breasts. I have spoken, declares the Sovereign LORD. 35 "Therefore this is what the Sovereign LORD says: Since you have forgotten me and thrust me behind your back, you must bear the consequences of your lewdness and prostitution." 36 The LORD said to me: "Son of man, will you judge Oholah and Oholibah? Then confront them with their detestable practices, 37 for they have committed adultery and blood is on their hands. They committed adultery with their idols; they even sacrificed their children, whom they bore to me, as food for them. 38 They have also done this to me: At that same time they defiled my sanctuary and desecrated my Sabbaths. 39 On the very day they sacrificed their children to their idols, they entered my sanctuary and desecrated it. That is what they did in my house. 40 "They even sent messengers for men who came from far away, and when they arrived you bathed yourself for them, painted your eyes and put on your jewelry. 41 You sat on an elegant couch, with a table spread before it on which you had placed the incense and oil that belonged to me. 42 "The noise of a carefree crowd was around her; Sabeans were brought from the desert along with men from the rabble, and they put bracelets on the arms of the woman and her sister and beautiful crowns on their heads. 43 Then I said about the one worn out by adultery, 'Now let them use her as a prostitute, for that is all she is.' 44 And they slept with her. As men sleep with a prostitute, so they slept with those lewd women, Oholah and Oholibah. 45 But righteous men will sentence them to the punishment of women who commit adultery and shed blood, because they are adulterous and blood is on their hands. 46 "This is what the Sovereign LORD says: Bring a mob against them and give them over to terror and plunder. 47 The mob will stone them and cut them down with their swords; they will kill their sons and daughters and burn down their houses. 48 "So I will put an end to lewdness in the land, that all women may take warning and not imitate you. 49 You will suffer the penalty for your lewdness and bear the consequences of your sins of idolatry. Then you will know that I am the Sovereign LORD."

Jeremiah 2

Israel Forsakes God

1 The word of the LORD came to me: 2 "Go and proclaim in the hearing of Jerusalem: " 'I remember the devotion of your youth, how as a bride you loved me and followed me through the desert, through a land not sown.

3 Israel was holy to the LORD, the firstfruits of his harvest; all who devoured her were held guilty, and disaster overtook them,' declares the LORD.

4 *Hear the word of the LORD, O house of Jacob, all you clans of the house of Israel. 5 This is what the LORD says: "What fault did your fathers find in me, that they strayed so far from me? They followed worthless idols and became worthless themselves. "*

Jeremiah 3

1 *"If a man divorces his wife and she leaves him and marries another man, should he return to her again? Would not the land be completely defiled? But you have lived as a prostitute with many lovers – would you now return to me?" declares the LORD. 6 During the reign of King Josiah, the LORD said to me, "Have you seen what faithless Israel has done? She has gone up on every high hill and under every spreading tree and has committed adultery there. 7 I thought that after she had done all this she would return to me but she did not, and her unfaithful sister Judah saw it. 8 I gave faithless Israel her certificate of divorce and sent her away because of all her adulteries. Yet I saw that her unfaithful sister Judah had no fear; she also went out and committed adultery. 9 Because Israel's immorality mattered so little to her, she defiled the land and committed adultery with stone and wood. 10 In spite of all this, her unfaithful sister Judah did not return to me with all her heart, but only in pretense," declares the LORD. 11 The LORD said to me, "Faithless Israel is more righteous than unfaithful Judah. 12 Go, proclaim this message toward the north: " 'Return, faithless Israel,' declares the LORD, 'I will frown*

on you no longer, for I am merciful,' declares the LORD, 'I will not be angry forever. 13 Only acknowledge your guilt – you have rebelled against the LORD your God, you have scattered your favors to foreign gods under every spreading tree, and have not obeyed me,' " declares the LORD. 14 "Return, faithless people," declares the LORD, "for I am your husband. I will choose you – one from a town and two from a clan – and bring you to Zion. 15 Then I will give you shepherds after my own heart, who will lead you with knowledge and understanding. 16 In those days, when your numbers have increased greatly in the land," declares the LORD, "men will no longer say, 'The ark of the covenant of the LORD.' It will never enter their minds or be remembered; it will not be missed, nor will another one be made. 17 At that time they will call Jerusalem The Throne of the LORD, and all nations will gather in Jerusalem to honor the name of the LORD. No longer will they follow the stubbornness of their evil hearts. 18 In those days the house of Judah will join the house of Israel, and together they will come from a northern land to the land I gave your forefathers as an inheritance.

Jer 31: 31 "The time is coming," declares the LORD, "when I will make a new covenant with the house of Israel and with the house of Judah. 32 It will not be like the covenant I made with their forefathers when I took them by the hand to lead them out of Egypt, because they broke my covenant, though I was a husband to them," declares the LORD.

Do we really believe God actually married these two whoring sisters? The two nations were His spiritual wives in type and shadow and in the metaphor of religious language. The metaphor was chosen because people of the time could relate to it easily. No one will dispute that in Old Testament times most leaders, kings, and men who could financially afford it had more than one wife.

According to the Torah or Old Testament, the law compelled Polygamy among God's people. It is interesting that in scripture there is a compulsion to have more than one wife. The command was not a specific command to have plural wives but polygamy had to occur as a consequence of obedience to another command, that a man was to raise up an heir for a dead relative. Keep in mind that this is God's command, through his prophet Moses, the proper name for the Law being "the Law of God, given to Moses." (Ezra 7:6, Nehemiah 10:29 & 2nd Chronicles 34:14) The law is described in Deuteronomy 25:5 (NASB) and says, when brothers live together and one of them dies and has no son, the wife of the deceased shall not be married outside the family to a strange man. Her husband's brother shall go in to her and take her to himself as wife and perform the duty of a husband's brother to her. It shall be that the firstborn whom she bears shall assume the name of his dead brother, so that his name will not be blotted out from Israel.

Deuteronomy 25:7 - 10 "But if the man does not desire to take his brother's wife, then his brother's wife shall go up to the gate to the elders and say, 'My husband's brother refuses to establish a name for his brother in Israel; he is not willing to perform the duty of a husband's brother to me.' Then the elders of his city shall summon him and speak to him. And if he persists and says, 'I do not desire to take her'. 9 his brother's widow shall go up to him in the presence of the elders, take off one of his sandals, spit in his face and say, "This is what is done to the man who will not build up his brother's family line." 10 That man's line shall be known in Israel as The Family of the Unsandaled."

1 Samuel 25:39 Then David sent word to Abigail, asking her to become his wife. 40 His servants went to Carmel and said to Abigail, "David has sent us to you to take you to become his wife." 41 She bowed down with her face to the ground and said, "Here is your maidservant, ready to serve you and wash the feet of my master's servants." 42 Abigail quickly got on a donkey and, attended by her five maids, went with David's messengers and became his wife. 43 David had also married Ahinoam of Jezreel, and they both were his wives. 44 But Saul had given his daughter Michal, David's wife, to Paltiel son of Laish, who was from Gallim.

1 Chronicles 4:5 Ashhur the father of Tekoa had two wives, Helah and Naarah.

2 Chronicles 11:22 Rehoboam appointed Abijah son of Maacah to be the chief prince among his brothers, in order to make him king. 23 He acted wisely, dispersing some of his sons throughout the districts of Judah and Benjamin, and to all the fortified cities. He gave them abundant provisions and took many wives for them.

Here we will resist going further, for to list all of the times multiple wives were recorded in the Old Testament would take up too much of this book.

Now we know that the Old Testament permitted polygamy and under certain circumstances, compels a man to take his brother's wife, if he should die, in order to continue his inheritance.

Where most casual Bible readers balk is in connecting polygamy to the New Testament. This is actually very simple and direct. Look at the NIV translation of the following verses.

1 Timothy 3
1Here is a trustworthy saying: If anyone sets his heart on being an overseer, he desires a noble task. 2Now the overseer must be above

reproach, the husband of but one wife, temperate, self-controlled, respectable, hospitable, able to teach, 3not given to drunkenness, not violent but gentle, not quarrelsome, not a lover of money. 4He must manage his own family well and see that his children obey him with proper respect. 5(If anyone does not know how to manage his own family, how can he take care of God's church?) 6He must not be a recent convert, or he may become conceited and fall under the same judgment as the devil. 7He must also have a good reputation with outsiders, so that he will not fall into disgrace and into the devil's trap. 8Deacons, likewise, are to be men worthy of respect, sincere, not indulging in much wine, and not pursuing dishonest gain. 9They must keep hold of the deep truths of the faith with a clear conscience. 10They must first be tested; and then if there is nothing against them, let them serve as deacons. 11In the same way, their wives are to be women worthy of respect, not malicious talkers but temperate and trustworthy in everything.

12A deacon must be the husband of but one wife and must manage his children and his household well. 13Those who have served well gain an excellent standing and great assurance in their faith in Christ Jesus.

For centuries, through the vague wording of the KJV Bible, this passage was used by some denominations to exclude all divorced men and every woman from the clergy. It is true that the phrase can be interpreted, "A bishop must be a one-woman

man." Some view the verse as a test for fidelity, pointing out
that polygamy was not the norm in the Greco-Roman world.
This is true but there was a great mixing of cultures and
increasing pagan and foreign influences being transmitted from
various sources. The Greco-Roman world was not the universe.
There were other cultures to consider. Those in the Middle
East, where Christ was born and crucified, had their own
customs.

First Timothy was written after the apostle Paul had been
imprisoned in Rome for the first time. After he was released, he
wrote this letter to Timothy, who by this time had served as a
son in the gospel with the apostle for several years. He was
probably in his late twenties or early thirties, and the apostle
had sent him to Ephesus, the great commercial and pleasure
resort on the shores of the Mediterranean in Asia Minor. In this
great crossroad and cultural melting pot all cultures would be
encountered and addressed.

Paul, being well educated and well traveled, would have
known the farther East one traveled the more polygamy would
be encountered. Many Bedouins, Arab tribes, and nomadic
people practice polygamy today. The meaning is made clear in
the NIV Bible. In the verses above we see the admonition to
limit one's household to a single wife if you wish to serve the

church. It is not that having more than one wife was a sin. Nowhere are we told that polygamy is wrong. We are only told that having more than one wife is not the optimum condition if one is to serve the church. The reason seems axiomatic. One cannot take the time and energy needed to keep up more than one household well and also serve the widows and orphans along with the church community. Jesus, living in a society permitting polygamy, never addressed it as a problem. Why do we? It is not because of our religion, but how we chose to interpret it through the blinders of our society.

We should never forget that many thousands of women choose polygamy, not because of any religious belief, but because it fits her needs. Family therapist Audrey Chapman wrote about non-Mormon American women that voluntarily chose a polygamous lifestyle. The women she interviewed told of safety, security and stability in their households. One woman remarked that she "knows at all times where her husband is." She also said, "I'm not worrying all the time that he's going to leave and break up my family." Another polygamous wife told Chapman that her relationship with a co-wife works because they don't see their husband as a possession. The wives in these households avoid rivalry by scheduling personal time with their husband and the husband including them in decision-making. A surprising revelation came from one wife when asked about their sex lives. While sexual contact is kept private and each wife respects that intimacy, she reported, "Actually not much sex occurs, because the relationship is not based on their physical union, but upon a spiritual basis instead." In this case, the word "spiritual" does not refer to a religion but a connection with the husband on a very personal level.

The evidence indicates that the great majority of American polygamists have not contributed to the cultural decay. By all accounts they are decent, hard-working and law-abiding citizens with strong moral, ethical and family values. One can only wonder how a man making a vow of lifetime fidelity, being responsible for the welfare of his wives and their children and teaching them to live by God's Word or a moral code can possibly be unhealthy or harm the women and children. Indeed, Christian and Fundamentalist Mormon polygamists seek to honor the principles of marriage found in the Bible just as committed Christian monogamists.

Polygamy / Polygyny – How it Works

Polygamy falls into two distinct categories. There is polygamy that is driven by religious belief and there is polygamy driven by secular or personal preference. Those of the secular kind come from an emotional disposition to gather and keep those people whom you love close, in a nurturing family. That is the healthy template. There are other reasons that are unhealthy. A man may collect women as one collects trophies. A man may also collect women as objects to dominate. Of course, women can do the same in regard to men.

Within the religious polygamy category we find the same functional and dysfunctional templates. Jewish, Christian, and Islamic traditions demand the husband treat each wife equally in regard to emotional and material, as well as sexual sufficiency. If a man cannot support a woman emotionally, materially, and sexually he should not marry. If he cannot support each wife equally in all areas he should not be a polygamist. Another consideration is time. There must not only be enough time for each wife individually but also for the children. In an ideal situation, the husband cared for by his family, would be able to meet the needs of more than one wife, as well as their offspring.

The accepted doctrine of the FLDS church indicates that if a man has less than three wives he will not see the highest realm of heaven. To reach the highest state and to be given a planet to lord over as God, he must have a minimum of three wives. The belief of the church states the Prophet Joseph Smith will be resurrected in the latter days. He will in turn resurrect the good Mormon men, who will in turn resurrect their favorite wives. Men faithful to the church and its doctrines and having at least three wives will be made gods and then given planets of their own over which to rule and reign. This belief puts the husband in a position of total sovereignty over the wives as their gateway to the afterlife. It also sets up an environment of competition and jealousy between the wives. The family unit becomes dysfunctional and poisonous if the wives are forced into competition with one another. Inevitably, jealousy and backbiting will spill onto the daughters because from generation to generation the females of the congregation are taught the doctrine. Husbands within the congregation could collect wives as talismans of power allowing the man to achieve godhood to rule over a planet.

Polygamy becomes a working family unit only when all members feel loved, honored and cherished. Each member should trust and be trusted. Each member should love and feel loved. Each member should care and be cared for. All the family members, in particularly the wives ,must have regular input on the workings of the family itself. Any other situation or environment that changes that state will doom the family to unhealthiness.

Polygamy can survive and thrive within the religious framework, if that framework is reasonable, balanced, and healthy. Most religious frameworks are patriarchal, which may be acceptable providing it is benevolent. The patriarch must put himself last. His life must be lived in service to those under his leadership. One person should never collect others to be in service to him or her in order to fulfill some quest of ego, sexual fantasy, or religious power.

There are logistical problems when it comes to a closed religious environment. Assuming that there only a 50 /50 split between the births of male and female children it becomes immediately obvious that there will be a dearth of females if each husband takes multiple wives. In the past, in a closed religious framework, the solution was for the older men with more power and authority in the religious setting, to oppose the younger males and drive them out of the community, taking more wives for themselves. As their age increased and their power and dominance within the religious community increased, they would take younger and younger wives. This would drive more and more of the young males out of the community, reducing the community to a small number of extended families.

In the environment of the US today, in an open society, polygamy may be the balancing point to correct the number of women who are unmarried as compared to the number of men. The percentages of unmarried women above the age of 40 continues to increase. Men tend to take younger brides. Women tend to outlive men. And so above the age of 40 there is a wider and wider discrepancy between the numbers of married women and married men. Since only a small percentage of women will find polygamy attractive it stands to reason that society as a whole would become more balanced and healthy if women and men who wished to live in this state of matrimony were allowed to do so.

Then the same mechanism of polygamy which destabilizes small closed communities could be used to balance society as a whole.

Why Would You Want To?

Although members of poly families may discuss issues with one another, because of an upswing in arrests and polarization of views it is be difficult to convince members to speak frankly on the record. Speaking up for the community in general was a woman we shall call "Dee". Dee was protective and loving regarding her way of life. She drew clear distinctions between those who "lord over and take advantage of their people in the name of religion" and those who, by their own choice, enter into a multiple marriage of their own free will because of love and commitment. When asked why she preferred to live in a polygyny marriage she listed the reasons in a series of one-word statements with explanations.

"Commitment – Each person is committed to the family and to one another.

Responsibility – There are strong, shared responsibilities assuring help and success.

Character – Even though those in monogamous relationships may not understand, we succeed and are happy only because we have enough love and character to overcome the pressure society places on us.

Equality – Each member is equal. In a working polygamous marriage it is the wives that are placed in the center. We have a say as to who is chosen as a wife. We must all be compatible and we must love each other like sisters. It is not a quick process. The hardest thing is not to allow selfishness or jealousy to divide the family. The second wife cannot be in second place.

Provision – Each of us contributes to the whole and there must always be enough to go around. It is sad that in the history of polygamy in the U.S. the hallmark has been poverty and loneliness for the wives. The husband, with input from the other wives, must be sure there will be enough money, time, and affection to go around. It is my personal belief a man cannot support more than three wives emotionally, even if he is a billionaire. Without love and time you do not really have a marriage. We are not concubines to be placed on the sidelines until he gets bored. We are fulltime wives. There are three states of relationships with multiple women and one man. You can be a girlfriend (if he is not married), the other woman (if he is married), or a wife. If God give us the blessing of love it should be done with respect.

Honor – Character and honor follow one upon the other, but

they are not the same. The husband and wives should honor the commitment of marriage. This means that a man should be careful not to let his ego or sex drive make his choices. He should never sink into a state where he would try to bring into the marriage a much younger woman. Men in monogamous marriages run off with younger women and leave their wives every day. It can be done within the plural marriage just as well, and he would not have to leave. All he would have to do is stop honoring his wives and his commitment. It takes a lot of trust on our side and great control and responsibility on his part. That is why the wives should have a voice in his choices. It keeps that kind of thing from happening. I think people like Jeffs and those other so-called leaders should be punished severely for what they do to those young girls. They have no honor.

We choose this way of life. It is a blessing to us. It is the large, extended family I wanted. It is the three-fold-cord that cannot be broken. It is a way to achieve balance in life with sister wives having good days and bad days and the one who is up helping the one who is down. It is the circle of friends and people we can count on in a world that is becoming more and more harsh and cruel. It is how I feel most comfortable living. "

The same rules would apply within the polyandry and polyamory relationships. Sex is important, but sex should never drive decisions. No one wants to marry a person they are not attached to, but if sex and attraction drive decisions there could be a time when the older wife is left out, or put aside, and that should never be. It is the deep and abiding love that will keep that kind of thing from happening.

Polyandry

Polyandry is a state of relationship where one woman has two or more husbands. Whereas Polygamy may work best to quickly grow a depleted population, Polyandry works best where there is poverty so severe that one adult male is not enough to provide for a wife and child. Of course, Polyandry is also a system best adopted in areas where there is a depleted population of females. This could occur for several reasons. Tribal conflicts can result in a conquest after which the women of the conquered tribe or nation are taken as slaves. Too many women dying in childbirth or from disease would reduce the female population. Infanticide of female babies, as practiced by some cultures also causes great imbalance.

Polyandry is generally found in areas where difficult physical environments or high populations impose extreme pressures on agricultural systems. It works to limit population growth and to ensure the coherence of agricultural estates.

The occurrence of Polyandry is rare and is concentrated in the Himalayan areas of South Asia. However, it is sporadically distributed in Africa, Polynesian countries, and Native America. Two forms have been recorded: fraternal polyandry in which a group of brothers share a wife, and non-fraternal polyandry in which a woman's husbands are not related. The non-fraternal form in the sense that a woman engages in sexual relations and has children with several different men, all of whom will be called upon to assist in support of the child and household. Fraternal forms are common in the mountainous areas of Nepal and Tibet. Among the Tibetian Nyinba, brothers live together throughout their lives in a large household kept within the inheritance of the brother-husbands. They share a common estate and domestic responsibilities. They also share a common wife with whom each maintains a sexual relationship. Polyandry, which is driven by sociological patterns, can be understood as a response to a shortage of women due to a lower survival rate in comparison to men or the mechanism by which family property, and thus valuable land used for farming or grazing, is kept within the family.

Polyandry has important implications in the areas of economics and inheritance. Since brothers share a wife, their joint estate remains intact from generation to generation. In an area or region where life revolves around an agrarian society, land is life. Fraternal Polyandry stops the division of land that usually occurs when children inherit only a share of the estate.

Some theorists suggest that this institution more often occurs in societies in which women hold relatively high social status. By marrying brothers the woman essentially doubles her estate and the inheritance of her children as compared to monogamous women.

Contained in a recent paper in the publication, *Human Nature,* co-authored by two anthropologists, Katherine Starkweather, a PhD candidate at the University of Missouri, and Raymond Hames, professor of anthropology at the University of Nebraska, is an unexpected insight into the history of polyandry.

The authors of the paper began a careful survey of the literature, and found anthropological accounts of 53 polyandrous societies *outside* of the well known societies such as Tibet. The anthropologists documented 53 social systems practicing polyandrous unions. They found societies described as, "among foragers in a wide variety of environments ranging from the Arctic to the tropics, and to the desert."

The researchers classified at least half these groups as hunter-gatherer societies and conclude that, if those groups are similar to our ancestors, as they suspected, then it is probable that polyandry has a deep human history.

The research suggests that "polyandry constitutes a variation on the common, evolutionarily-adaptive phenomenon of pair-bonding -- a variation that sometimes emerges in response to environmental conditions."

What kind of environmental conditions? Well, "classical polyandry" in Asia has allowed families in areas of scarce farmable land to hold agricultural estates together. The marriage of all brothers in a family to the same wife allows plots of family-owned land to remain intact and undivided." This may not seem important in our society, but if one extrapolates how a parcel of land, which provides only subsistence farming for a family, would be divided into ever-diminishing and smaller lots as families have children and sons take their portions for their inheritance, it becomes apparent that within a generation or two land allowed such sub-divisions would not support even the smallest family.

In other cultures, a man may arrange a second husband (again, frequently his brother) for his wife because he knows that, when he must be absent, the second husband will protect his interests. If she becomes pregnant the child is still considered related by blood and by an approved father.

Anthropologists have recorded this kind of situation among certain cultures among the Inuit (Eskimos). Eskimos were also known to share their wife with visitors to better forge lasting alliances. Something necessary in such a hostile environment.

The Bari people of Venezuela recognize two living men as fathers of a single child. Children understood to have two fathers are significantly more likely to survive to age 15 than children with only one. This is called the "father effect."

Some older cultures, which are without the benefit of modern science, believe that the fetuses is the result of multiple contributions of semen over the course of a pregnancy, as if the semen builds the fetus. This concept is called "partible paternity" and is a result of a form of "informal polyandry." It is termed "informal" because both fathers may not be formally married to and living with the woman but the society officially recognizes both men as legitimate fathers to her child.

In all polyandrous systems women may openly have multiple mates simultaneously. Women in such systems are not cheating or committing adultery, nor are the men raising children under the guise of exclusivity. The systems are socially sanctioned.

One would assume these societies are matriarchal but that is not usually the case. It is the first husband who functions as the manager of resource distribution and selection of any additional male mates.

It is true that humans appear prone to sexual jealousy, which would make poly-unions untenable. Anthropologists have found that in both polyandry (one woman, multiple husbands) and polygyny (one husband, multiple wives), sexual jealousy often functions as a stressor in families around the world, yet when environmental or emotional circumstances prevail individuals and cultures adapt. When fertile women are scarce, men are more likely to be found openly sharing women. Three-quarters of the 53 societies identified by Starkweather and Hames involve skewed sex ratios, with more adult males than females.

Polyandry shows up mostly in relatively egalitarian societies. These are societies with very simple social structures, without massive governmental bureaucracies and elaborate class structures. This is why polyandry is regularly found among the South American Yanomamö, the people Hames studied in the field in the 1970s and 1980s. But other places where there are skewed ratios of men and women, such as modern India and China, are not simple egalitarian societies. Changes in such regulated societies come slowly and not without social upheaval.

In the chaos of the founding of the Mormon (LDS) church, 11 of Joseph Smith's first 33 wives were married to other men. Smith asked to be sealed or married to them, thus entering into polyandrous relationships with 11 women.

In societies where the wealth is in the land or where male children are valued higher than female children there will likely be an excess of men at one point or another. Societies have dealt with this by sending the excess men into the priesthood, the military, or simply forced them out of mainstream society via colonization and exploration. This tends to be a solution but polyandry may still occur in various and unsanctioned ways.

A survey of traditional societies in the world, quoted in Psychology Today, Published on June 5, 2008, showed that "83.39% of the societies practice polygyny, 16.14% practice monogamy, and .47% practice polyandry. Almost all of the few polyandrous societies practice what anthropologists call *fraternal polyandry*, where a group of brothers share a wife. Non-fraternal polyandry, where a group of unrelated men share a wife, is virtually nonexistent in human society."

The term "Traditional Society" is usually contrasted with industrial, urbanized, capitalist 'modern' society. Traditional society is quite formal. People's names are indicators of social status. There is usually a cast or social system of hierarchy. Sons tend to follow in the father's footsteps and discipline. If your father was a carpenter you will be one also.

There is a strong sense of morality and religious law that is shared by members of the community. The impersonal or modern society is much more informal.

In a traditional society the family name is linked to cast or social placement. Traditional society focuses more towards the improvement of society as a whole rather than focusing on self and personal gain.

The economics in a traditional society are focused on need, food, and supply, rather than gain. A member of traditional society would be opposed to producing crops or items for profit growth because in traditional society the main reasons for production were for use and subsistence. They produced to survive so there wouldn't have been a need for all of the excess that modern society produces in order to increase profits. There is little accumulation in a traditional society. Because traditional societies tend to move as a group, having something that others did not would lead to imbalance and disruption. In traditional societies, materials were seen as resources to help with the survival of the society as a whole.

Countries which would be examples of this would be many of the African countries which use agriculture as their main basis for growing food and for jobs. In addition some Asian countries, such as Bangladesh and Burma also rely on farming (agriculture) as their main way for both employment and for producing food for the family and the nation.

It is within these traditional societies that over 83% have some form of "poly" practices.

Lest we think this behavior odd, it would be good to first consider that the modern world has its share of polygamy, in the form of multiple consenting partners, in the order of up to 100,000 families. This in no way includes multiple partners in the form of what society considers adultery.

In Psychology Today, June 2008, Satoshi Kanazawa explains: "The estimates for cuckoldry (where the man unknowingly raises another man's genetic child) *in monogamous societies* range from 13-20% in the United States, 10-14% in Mexico, and 9-17% in Germany. This means one out of every five American fathers may be unwittingly raising someone else's child, erroneously believing it to be genetically his child. This is what I referred to as "unsanctioned polyandry."

When multiple men are officially married to one woman, who is "supposed to" mate with all of them, the co-husbands have very little reason to believe that a given child of hers is genetically his, and will therefore not be very motivated to invest in it. If the children receive insufficient paternal investment, they will not survive long enough to become adults and continue the society. Non-fraternal polyandry therefore contains the seeds of its own extinction.

In contrast, fraternal polyandry, where the co-husbands are brothers, can survive as a marriage institution because even when a given husband is not the genetic father of a given child (sharing half of his genes), he is at least the genetic uncle (sharing a quarter of his genes). The child of a fraternal polyandrous marriage could never be completely genetically unrelated to any of the co-husbands (assuming, of course, that the wife has not mated with anyone outside of the polyandrous marriage), so all the co-husbands are motivated to invest in all the children, either as their genetic father or their genetic uncle.

In other words, just as it is in the animal kingdom, males are programmed to raise their own children and thus continue their own genetic code. This is actually proven by the work of Professor Gordon G. Gallup, Jr. and his collaborators at the State University of New York - Albany. Gallup's work shows the shape of the human penis to be "quite distinct from that of many other primate species. In particular, the gland ("head") of the human penis is shaped like a wedge. The diameter of the posterior gland is larger than the penis shaft itself, and the coronal ridge, which rises at the interface between the gland and the shaft, is positioned perpendicular to the shaft.

In addition, the human male during copulation engages in repeated thrusting motions before he ejaculates. The combined effect of the particular shape of the penis gland and the repeated thrusting motions during intercourse is to draw foreign semen back away from the cervix. If a female copulated with more than one male within a short period of time, this would allow subsequent males to "scoop out" semen left by others before ejaculating. In other words, according to Gallup, the human penis is a "semen displacement device." It is designed and used to remove other men's semen from the cervix before the man ejaculates." Human males are built to better assure the offspring he raises is his own. Of course, this also proves that females may copulate with more than one male in a short period of time.

Satoshi Kanazawa, in a tongue in cheek article in Psychology Today asked the question (and then answers it); "So how do we know that women have not been sexually exclusive to their husbands throughout human evolutionary history? It turns out that clear evidence of women's promiscuity has been left on the man's body, his genitals, to be precise.

The first piece of evidence is the relative size of the testes. Across species, the more promiscuous the females are, the larger the size of the testes relative to the male's body weight. This is because when a female copulates with multiple males within a short period of time -- in other words, when she is promiscuous -- sperm from different males must compete with each other to reach the egg to inseminate it. This process is known as "sperm competition." One good way to outcompete others is to outnumber them. Male gorillas, whose females live in a harem tightly controlled by one silverback male and therefore do not have many opportunities for extra-pair copulations ("affairs"), have relatively small testes (0.02% of body weight) and produce a very small number of sperm per ejaculate (50 million). They don't have to produce a lot of sperm to impregnate their females because their sperm are not likely competing with anyone else's.

On the other extreme, male chimpanzees, whose females are highly promiscuous and do not attach themselves to any single male (in other words, they don't have "pair-bonding") have relatively large testes (0.3% of body weight) and produce a very large number of sperm per ejaculate (600 million). So, compared to gorillas, chimpanzees have testes 15 times as large, and produce 12 times as many sperm per ejaculate. They have to, if they have any hope of outnumbering sperm from other males and inseminating the egg before them.

On this scale, humans lie somewhere between the gorilla and the chimpanzee, but closer to the former than the latter. Men's testes are about 0.04% to 0.08% of their body weight, and the approximate number of sperm per ejaculate is 250 million. So women have been more promiscuous than gorilla females in their evolutionary history, but not nearly as promiscuous as chimpanzee females. The evidence of women's promiscuity throughout evolutionary history is in the relative size of men's testicles. Men would not have such large testicles and produce so many sperm per ejaculate had women not been so promiscuous. But then, their testicles would have been much larger and they would have produced even more sperm per ejaculate had women been more promiscuous."

So, men can never be sure if the child of their mate is indeed their own. The male must continually and consciously over ride the internal push in order to fairly and properly raise another man's child. When the data is uncertain in the mind of the male as to if there is a genetic connection to the child the male has primal emotional confusion.

Because of the conflicting emotional impulses of needing to continue society and the urge of the male to continue familial genetic continuity, polyandry is brought to a virtual standstill.

Polyandry took place in a religious setting at the beginning of the Mormon Church. As Joseph Smith began to marry more and more women, he crossed into polyandry by marrying women who were already married and continued to be married to her first husband. Brigham Young continued this behavior.

In the system of Mormon polyandry, practiced in Nauvoo and later in Utah, polyandrous marriages were limited to male-initiated relationships. Polyandry was usually permitted for those well established in leadership positions within the church. In this Orwellian world the pigs got all the apples.

The fact that women had little to no say in the arrangements placed additional an emotional burden on the women, who were systematically coerced into the relationship. Allowing for informal female-initiated polyandry would help ameliorate the feelings of betrayal, but in a male-driven institution allowing women the power of choice would be out of the question.

Since this type of polyandry was not fraternal there would be times it could result in loss of status for participating women if they were forced to marry men of unequal status or if there were resentments by the first husband. Another consequence would be the social stigma attached to women who sleep with more than one man. Polyandry could have serious negative social consequences if it were not the norm.

In societies where there is no choice for women in the marriage arrangements, the situation often comes down to the dynamic of multiple men competing for sexual access to attractive women.

The story of Zina Diantha Huntington Jacobs Smith Young is part of the Mormon history. She was a pretty woman who twice entered into polyandrous marriages; at least one of them caused her quite a bit of anguish. She received a polyandrous marriage proposal from Joseph Smith while she was married to Henry Jacobs. She struggled with this idea, writing that it was a greater sacrifice than giving her life; ultimately she acquiesced only when Joseph told her that an angel would slay him if she did not marry him. (ISL, 80-81).

She writes less about her polyandrous marriage to Brigham Young, but notes that she felt "weakness of heart" after it. (Id. at 85-86). Zina continued in her marriage to Mr. Jacobs, but the additional relationship added stress and pain to the primary marriage.

In a society where polyandry is accepted and women were allowed to choose their mates this institution would provide expanded emotional and sexual expression for women.

Polyamory

Polyamory, also called "plural marriage," is less common than polygyny, but much more popular than polyandry. Polyamory is not driven by religious beliefs, unlike many occurrences of polygyny. Polyamory is likely to be produced when couples or families come together, deciding they have love, interests, and emotional connections in common.

In an article from Newsweek Magazine, titled, "Only You. And You. And You", published July 28, 2009, polyamory was examined from the viewpoint of a practicing family unit.

Excerpts taken from the article stated; "Researchers are just beginning to study the phenomenon of polyamory. Those who have began to research estimate that openly polyamorous families in the United States number more than half a million, with thriving contingents in nearly every major city.

"There have always been some loud-mouthed ironclads talking about the labors of monogamy and multiple-partner relationships," says Ken Haslam, a retired anesthesiologist who curates a polyamory library at the Indiana University-based Kinsey Institute for Research in Sex, Gender and Reproduction. "But finally, with the Internet, the thing has really come about."

With polyamorists' higher profile has come some growing pains. The majority of them don't seem particularly interested in pressing a political agenda; the joke in the community is that the complexities of their relationships leave little time for activism. But they are beginning to show up on the radar screen of the religious right, some of whose leaders have publicly condemned polyamory as one of a host of deviant behaviors sure to become normalized if gay marriage wins federal sanction.

"This group is really rising up from the underground, emboldened by the success of the gay-marriage movement," says Glenn Stanton, the director of family studies for Focus on the Family, an evangelical Christian group. "And while there's part of me that says, 'Oh, my goodness, I don't think I could see them make grounds,' there's another part of me that says, 'Well, just watch them.'"

Anecdotally, research shows that children can do well in polyamorous families—as long as they're in a stable home with loving parents, says Elisabeth Sheff, a sociologist at Georgia

State University, who is conducting the first large-scale study of children of polyamorous parents, which has been ongoing for a decade. But because academia is only beginning to study the phenomenon — Sheff's study is too recent to have drawn conclusions about the children's well-being over time — there is little data to support that notion in court.

Today, the nonprofit Polyamory Society posts a warning to parents on its Web site: *If your PolyFamily has children, please do not put your children and family at risk by coming out to the public or by being interviewed [by] the press!*

The notion of multiple-partner relationships is as old as the human race itself. But polyamorists trace the foundation of their movement to the utopian Oneida commune of upstate New York, founded in 1848 by Yale theologian John Humphrey Noyes. Noyes believed in a kind of communalism he hoped would fix relations between men and women; both genders had equal voice in community governance, and every man was considered to be married to every woman. But it wasn't until the late-1960s and 1970s "free love" movement that polyamory truly came into vogue; when books like *Open Marriage* topped best-seller lists and groups like the North American Swingers Club began experimenting with the concept. The term "polyamory," coined in the 1990s, popped up in both the

Merriam-Webster and Oxford English dictionaries in 2006.

Polyamory might sound like heaven to some: a variety of partners, adding spice and a respite from the familiarity and boredom that's doomed many traditional couples. But humans are hard-wired to be jealous, and though it may be possible to overcome it, polyamorous couples are "fighting Mother Nature" when they try, says biological anthropologist Helen Fisher, a professor at Rutgers University who has long studied the chemistry of love. Polyamorists say they aren't so much denying their biological instincts as insisting they can work around them — through open communication, patience, and honesty. Polyamorists call this process "compersion" — or learning to find personal fulfillment in the emotional and sexual satisfaction of your partner, even if you're not the one doing the satisfying. "It's about making sure that *everybody's* needs are met, including your own," says Terisa. "And that's not always easy, but it's part of the fun."

It's complicated, to say the least: tending to the needs of multiple partners, figuring out what to tell the kids, making sure that nobody's feelings are hurt. "I like to call it poly*agony*," jokes Haslam, the Kinsey researcher, who is himself polyamorous. "It works for some perfectly, and for others it's a disaster."

It's easy to dismiss polyamory as a kind of frat-house fantasy gone wild. But in truth, the community has a decidedly feminist bent: women have been central to its creation, and "gender equality" is a publicly recognized tenet of the practice."

End Excerpts

What is the advantage of Polyamory? If the household is stable and balanced, polyamory shields the members from the full repercussions of the sickness, injury, desertion, or death of a partner. This process will usually be more of a boon for the females in the group.

Many times women are left in poverty with little hope of continuing an established lifestyle if their husband becomes absent for any reason. If the husband becomes ill or is injured the process accelerates as she struggles alone to care for him with reduced income. In a polyamorous household there are resources to draw on that would assist in times of need, whether the need is emotional, financial, or physical. The remaining male or males can provide strength and income that would normally become absent with the death of a single husband.

Likewise, if a wife were to die, the other women in the

relationship, having already established emotional and sexual ties, could provide much needed comfort for the remainder of his life.

The children in a Polyamorous environment have more protection and assistance than a standard family. More resources are brought to bear and if the family unit is stable the situation emulates some American Indian philosophy stated as; "It takes a Tribe to raise a child."

If a parent dies, although no one can replace a connection between child and parent, there would be a system in place to love and raise the child and ease their grief, helping them transition into a life without one of their biological parents.

The natural resistance of jealousy is the obstacle for polyamory, polyandry, and polygyny. Some will maneuver the minefield better than others.

Sex

In the vast majority of poly relationships sex is kept between a husband and a wife. It is the norm in a polygamous / polygyny relationship that each wife has her own space, like a small apartment within the main home. It is her bed that the husband visits. This space is personal, private, and sacred to her alone. There is no worry about sharing the bed with another wife.

The husband and wives work out a schedule for intimacy. Given, this does reduce spontaneity at times but so does our work-a-day life. The husband visits his wives on a schedule and may stay with them for a night or series of nights. Each wife gets equal time. If sickness occurs the schedule picks up after a time where it ceased last.

Another way of working the schedule is for a common calendar to be placed in a shared space, such as the kitchen. Wives can schedule time as they need and want. This approach works better for those whose schedules may change due to work hours or having to travel on business.

Some families leave the scheduling of private time as a spontaneous choice. This is not recommended. It is human nature to be sexually attracted to one more than another, may be preferred for intellectual qualities. Allowing a totally free choice will in time show preferences to one person or another, seeding jealousy and resentment.

Although it is not unheard of, seldom do two women share a bed with the husband. Yet, in all the wedding bed is undefiled whatever the personal choices may be.

In a relationship of polyandry most cultures have the men living apart and visiting the wife in what is termed a "walking marriage." Of the few polyandrous relationships in the U.S. this is not always the case and two or more men may share a house with a single woman. In such cases the woman may visit the man of her choice or invite him into her bedroom.

When it comes to intimacy, there are no rules except those agreed upon by the individuals, or in the case of religiously based polygamy, those rules set forth by the doctrines and leaders.

It is quite uncommon in the setting of religiously based polygamy for a man to be with more than one woman at a time. It is considered immoral and disrespectful.

Within a secular, non-religious setting the rules are established based on the needs, happiness, and comfort of each individual. Or at least it should be. If it is not the pressure of the discomfort will damage the relationships and the family group.

The Logistics of Running Poly Households

**From each according to his ability,
to each according to his needs.   Karl Marx**

One of the main and most important issues relating to polygamy, in all its forms, is the configuration of the household. How does the traditional household add another person? What happens if there are children being intergraded? Is it best for multiple spouses to have separate homes or is it best for the family to live together, each having a separate section of the house. In smaller dwellings, do the wives have separate areas or simply separate rooms? How is the money divided among the members of the household? Does it matter if one works and one does not? What if one wife makes a great deal more money than the other? Does it matter if the husband works or not? Are members allowed to have their own personal savings account? What about cases of retirement or divorce (or in the case where a non-legal spouse leaves)? These questions are very important.

How are the kids raised? Are all adult members looked at as

parents or do the biological parents carry more authority?

How will time for dating and sex be arranged between multiple spouses?

Out of the vast numbers of divorces, sex, money, and parenting styles top the charts for reasons causing arguments and ultimately the dissolution of marriages. Multiply the percentages by the number of spouses and we have a recipe for disaster. Sadly, there is no perfect solution or answer to any of the questions posed. Each member has his or her needs and each person needs certain degrees of financial, physical, and emotional security. Each arrangement has its benefits and pitfalls, but if the pros and cons are weighed and balanced each family can reach the best solution for their unit.

Many poly households are being supported by U.S. citizens. Many of whom do not agree with the institution. Since only one of the marriages are legal, the wives and children of the illegal marriages are listed as being supported by an unwed mother. Welfare pays the mother to support her and her children. If polygamy were to be made legal this loophole would be closed. The other wives and children could be covered by the husband's insurance and Medicaid would be spared the extra drain. Insurance could revise family plans to charge per member, saving some money and charging others for their larger families.

Think deeply, think broadly, and think ahead. In the running of a poly household there are complexities expanding exponentially with the number of members and children.

Most poly households have a core built around a "first couple" of a husband and wife who are legally married. This means, in the case of polygamous relationships within joint property states, such as Alabama, if the husband were to die all property, houses, and belongings would go to the first wife. In households where there is a single dwelling, housing multiple wives and children, the estate would belong to the legal wife alone. The other wives and children must trust her to continue the family with equity. Although wills may be contested in court, it is best for all parties to have a will specifying how to distribute property and wealth.

In spite of the inherent issues of having a single dwelling, this seems to be the most financially feasible of all options, and the one allowing better emotional connect between members. There would be only a single structure to maintain. There would be a single bill for electricity and so forth. Time and energy would be conserved. This will become more important as the couples age. In times where one wife or husband is ill others would be close by. Older children could assist with the younger children and help with chores.

The house should be set up to allow each member to have some personal space for rest, meditation, study, hobbies, and relaxation. Emotional and mental health becomes a growing issue when living among a group.

If wives have their own homes it leads to material security, with each wife knowing she owns her own home and has her own space but the upkeep and bills expand accordingly. Since repairs and upkeep usually fall to the husband to do he could become overwhelmed, stressed and exhausted. A bit more added to the common fund for hiring a handyman to help would be a good idea for situations where wives live in separate houses.

For poly households there are a myriad of situations to consider. Should all the wives work? Should there be one who stays home and runs the household, shuttles the children, and prepares meals? How is that person to be compensated?

If wives are working, how is the income divided? Does each person contribute a certain amount or a certain percentage of income of their income to the household? If one person makes only four-hundred dollars a week and another makes two-thousand dollars a week should they pay into the common fund the same amount or the same percentage of their income?

If one wife has 1 child and another has 4 children it would make sense to give her more money to provide for them. Should there be a common pool of money accessible by all wives and husbands?

One way to distribute funds in a poly household is for wives to work in their preferred professions and contribute a certain amount to a single fund.

For single dwelling households a common fund is almost essential. Each wife would work in her chosen discipline. One wife would stay home to keep house, care for children and prepare meals. In larger families more than one housewife may be required. Each working member should contribute either a percent of her income or a certain amount of income. The common pool would pay for the household food, upkeep and bills, as well as the transportation for all. The stay-at-home wives must be compensated as well. Each member should have their own discretionary income for personal items, clothing, and the like. A life of polygamy should not equate to poverty or austerity.

If wives have their own homes, wives would pay for their homes and children. The common fund would be used to pay the wife who wishes to stay home, run errands and shuttle the children. The fund would also be used for upkeep of houses and cars.

Each wife and husband should have the ability to save money for themselves and for security.

With trust and love ruling the situation the most direct and simple solution to the financial issue would apply. All members living in a common and well designed home would share a common pool of money is order to support the entire household as a common unit. Each member would be allowed a certain amount per month for personal discretion. Children would be well clothed and fed. Bills would be paid. Maintenance would be done. What is left after each month would be moved to a common savings account.

Home and Housing

Every individual needs a safe and personal space. We want to belong to a tight knit family. We want and need to be alone from time to time. Both environments should be provided and accessible at the same time. How to do this is one of the puzzles for individuals in "poly" families. To do so in the most efficient and effective way is one of the basic quandaries.

There are several possibilities for how to set up housing. Each member can live in their own homes. Members can all live together in a single dwelling. Some can live in one home and others in a second or third house. Each configuration presents problems and advantages.

The most efficient accommodation is for all members to live in a single house. One house payment and a single structure to keep in repair will decrease both financial and physical output. The home should be large enough for each member to have their own areas. If it is possible, break the house into stand alone apartments with a large central kitchen and family area for full family fun, meetings and meals. This will provide the personal space and the family environment needed.

Resources – Time is Money

If only one person in the extended family contributes financially to the household the configuration of finances is the simplest it can be, which, with multiple spouses, is difficult enough. One bank account does not mean one controller. The family must decide who will control the flow of money and how funds will be distributed. If several people have access to accounts there must be a central way of coordinating funds.

After bills, utilities, and mortgage or rent are all paid, each person must have a reasonable amount of discretionary income for clothing and items used for "individualization," an important quality to keep the group healthy.

If we are forward-thinking we will prepare for the future. Some money must be put back in case of unforeseen problems, sickness, or disaster. What is just as important is the prospect of retirement of the main provider. Preparations will effect many people, and with children being involved the outcome will effect many more. With the possibility of default within the Social Security system in the U.S., it becomes even more important to talk about and plan for the future. A plan should be laid out so the family unit can be made the most efficient and cost effective as possible.

When death occurs within the family vested parties may begin to bicker. If left up to all parties, surviving spouses could turn against one another or choose to leave with the funds and his or her biological children. Human nature being what it tends to be, it is best to form a trust with a disinterested party such as an attorney with no former ties to anyone in the group.

There is an established group near my home, the members of which I know. The trust structure they came up with is intriguing. No one owns land. The trust owns the property. This keeps resources safely within the family. If, for example a wife leaves or divorces the family, under normal circumstances she would be entitled to part of the land. Now, let us imagine that a year or so later she marries a man hostile to the remaining family. Under the law of state that are common or community property state he would also own the land given to the estranged ex-wife. Worse yet, if the wife died the new husband becomes the owner of the property. Now, in the middle of the land once held intact by the family is a plot of land owned by a hostile person. Life would become "interesting."

To keep this scenario from taking place the trust owns the land

and members lease the property for a specified length of time. Children of members are afforded the opportunity to continue the lease after the death of a parent, provided they follow the by-laws laid down by the group. Leases may be terminated if by-laws are not kept. This approach seems cold and surgical, but rules keep order, which is important in a large and expanding family group. Soon enough the family becomes a group and the group becomes a community. The Mormons went through this evolution. Laws and doctrine formed accordingly.

Resources

Money, and the sheer lack of resources plague many polygamist families. As the family grows and children are born our most precious resource, time, is taxed.

Consider a normal schedule. The husband and / or wife arise at 6 A.M., gets the kids ready for school and leaves for work. The average commute time in the U.S. is about 25 minutes. The parent leaves work around 5 P.M. and arrives home at 5:30. Supper must be prepared and eaten. Minor repairs of house and property must be preformed. On a large home or several smaller homes upkeep, repair, and lawn work could demand more time than anticipated. Usually there are several cars owned by a large family. With stretched resources the cars may be older and more likely to need repair. Bills must be paid. Children must be taken on outings, as well as to doctor and dentist appointments.

Multiple children need time with the father, help with homework, and social issues at school. Extracurricular activities run rampant when that family has many children. Keeping schedules in sync with several games, practices, and performances become difficult. Other children will be pulled in to provide transportation. Mother and Father cannot attend more than one event a day. More sensitive children will feel left out. This is a mine field one must cross in order to be successful in a multiple marriage.

To avoid the extracurricular minefield and the feeling that mom and dad are missing from the various events it may be suitable to forgo school activities in favor of family outings where parents and children can bond while having fun as a group. Children need to socialize outside the family, so include a few of their friends if possible. After all, what more disruption can a few more children cause in such a large brood of chicks?

With the gap of the "connected and unconnected" households growing, it is necessary to have computers and internet connection so all children can do their best in school.

In a traditional family of 2.5 kids there are days where parents must stay home with the child due to illness. Multiply the number 3 times or more and there will be many days missed at work by one parent or another.

It becomes apparent that in larger units it is best to have a "stay at home parent."

According to the federal government, the U.S. national **average wage** index for 2010 was $41,673.83.

    NEW YORK (CNNMoney) reports, "Just providing a child with the basics has become more than most parents can afford."

The cost of raising a child from birth to age 18 for a middle-income, two-parent family averaged $226,920 last year (not including **college**), according to the U.S. Department of Agriculture. That's up nearly 40% -- or more than $60,000 -- from 10 years ago. Just one year of spending on a child can cost up to $13,830 in 2010, compared to $9,860 a decade ago.

Many parents are working longer hours, or another job, and they are giving up time at home. It's a complete catch-22. From buying groceries to paying for gas, every major expense associated with raising a child has climbed significantly over the past decade.

Food prices, in particular, have weighed on parents' budgets as rising demand for commodities like corn and wheat, along with other factors such as rising oil prices, drought and floods, have made even a box of cereal a pricey proposition. Another notable increase has been the cost of transportation, which soared as a result of rising gas prices. Between 2000 and 2010, consumers paid an average of 85% more per gallon at the pump, according to AAA.

The battered economy has also taken a toll, of course. Many employers scaled back or even did away with medical coverage in recent years, leaving many families to cover that bill. At the same time, costs for doctors visits, medications and other health services also climbed. As a result, health care costs for families with children rose 58% over the decade.

All of this comes at a time when incomes are shrinking and unemployment is near an all-time high. Over the past decade, **median household income** has fallen 7%, according to a recent report from the Census Bureau.

The early years are among the toughest for parents who must find a way to afford all of those costs, plus child care.
"It takes half of my paycheck to pay for my child care -- you start to feel like, is this even worth it?" said Anna Aasen, a mother of two from Roseburg, Ore.

Although housing generally represents a family's largest expense, putting more than one child in day care tips the scales.

The anti-baby boom: Why the U.S. Birth Rate Keeps Falling

In 2010, the cost of putting two children in child care exceeded the median annual rent payments in every single state, according to a recent report by the National Association of Child Care Resource & Referral Agencies, or NACCRRA.

"It defies logic," said Linda Smith, NACCRRA's executive director. As more families are priced out of licensed child care services, the health and safety of those children are put in jeopardy, she said.
Licensed day care for two children can comprise more than 25% of a an average annual income.

End of NACCRRA Article

If placing 2 children in daycare can take over a quarter of the average income, imagine the cost of placing as many children as is possible from a multiple family. Again, we return to the need of having at least one adult member of the family at home as a parent and administrator of the household.

Economy of Scale

Looking at just a few of the problems listed above, one can see where the letters of the original Mormon women could serve as a warning beacon to those who would enter into polygamy without counting the cost in time and money. When advanced over more than two or three wives of child-bearing age the economy of scale falls apart rapidly as one considers the mere drain of resources in properly parenting and raising dozens of children. Resources must be considered. Women may wish to restrict the number of their biological children to two or three each, keeping the family to a manageable size.

Having one, two or three wives with a set limit of children, all living under one roof, with one of the wives as a stay at home mom to manage the household and small children seems to be the best overall solution for most of the problems that will be encountered in a polygamist lifestyle. Two wives may be the optimum number, at least for us. We came to this revelation because only two wives can be close to the husband at the same time. We have two arms with which to embrace. A third wife would always be on the outside of a hug or snuggle.

The stumbling blocks of jealousy, strife, proper divisions of labor, distribution of resources and the need for individual time and money for the adult members will still have to be worked out.

Considering many of the problems a young family will have to overcome, as counter-intuitive as it may seem, polygamy may fare better and be of greater service to older men and women. Polyandry should also be considered.

Older members would have raised their children and would not have to worry about the problems of limited time. With the cost of living rising rapidly, a single household with combined income and divided housing and energy costs would help provide an overall decrease in cost per member.

Even more needful are the watchful eyes and helpful assistance for those who may be infirmed in some way. For elderly members polygamy offers a huge number of benefits.

Considering a more pragmatic approach to life, the problems of jealousy and divisions of income would be less of a problem. Each member would have retirement or social security income and would simply contribute a portion toward the running of the household. Children and the costs of activities beyond the household would be less of a concern.

Even though the lifespan of men are slowly catching up with that of women, ladies are still likely to outlive men.

With a household designed around polyamory of two or three men and one to three women, the mix would be right to continue the arrangement with its benefits in the event some men die before the female members. This fact alone makes polyandry another reasonable alternative.

Downfalls and Traps - The Undoing

Certain facts cannot be overstated, nor can they be stated often enough. There are several traps to avoid if a family is to be happy with and in polygyny or polyandry.

Before the first marriage, if one of the spouses wishes to expand the marriage into polygamy the spouse should announce this to their intended spouse at the beginning. Using the husband as an example, if after being married for several years he revealed his desire for another wife his wishes could be construed as a breach of an emotional or a marital contract. Resistance, and emotions of resentment and betrayal would result. Likewise, if the husband feels deeply in his heart polygamy is where he belongs, the refusal on the part of the first wife will be viewed as a limitation and denial of his happiness and fulfillment. This scenario is the first and greatest problem to avoid. People change. Insight expands. Polygamy may be entertained later on in a marriage, but when it comes up be prepared for the reactions and talk it through carefully and with mutual respect.

If someone wishes to sleep with more than one person, it is much simpler solution to just stay single.

If polygamy is decided on and a second wife is found, do not be surprised if in getting your wish you may not get what you wanted. He who rides a tiger dares not dismount. There will be stresses and demands. Simply put, one person becomes the emotional focus of several people. The husband, in the case of polygyny, and the wife, in the case of polyandry, must supply enough emotional content, time and sex for all spousal members. If this is not accomplished the result is loneliness.

Each person must be made to feel special, as if they are the only one existing, especially in those times of intimacy. It must be personal and fulfilling. Attention of the husband, in the case of polygyny, must be like a spotlight illuminating the spirit of the wife in their time of togetherness.

All members must be financially and materially supplied. No one should be without adequate food, clothing, transportation, and housing.

In this modern world transportation is very important. No one should be left alone with children without transportation. It is simply not safe when one factors in all accidents and sickness possible in large households.

Polygamy can be very expensive and demanding. If one cannot afford it financially and emotionally they should not attempt it.

If all members should have the same general accoutrements and quality of life the money for members making less than others must come from a common fund administered in a socialist type arrangement. If the fund is lacking it usually falls to the husband to financially make up for financial shortcoming of wives who make less than others or are stay-at-home wives. It is also up to him to manage upkeep of the property.

Realizing this may sound sexist to many, one must keep in mind the basis for polygyny for many people is a very conservative religious indoctrination.

No matter what style of polygamy is practiced, the major complaints of women in plural marriages is loneliness and poverty. Why? Because their husbands married more women or had more children than they could care for. A man does not do his wives any favors by marrying them if he cannot be with them enough or support them in good fashion. Even if one believes as the FLDS church teaches, that unmarried adults cannot reach the highest glory, the hell of poverty and loneliness here is unnecessary if the husband is kind, fair, and sensible. Furthermore, the FLDS idea that the primary purpose of wives in a plural marriage is to give birth to children in order to populate God's kingdom seems on the surface to diminish the scope and depth of the human spirit. Over population within a family has the same complications as over population within a nation. Scarce resources, poverty, ill health, and malnutrition. Impregnating a wife and leaving her to raise the child with minimum help is not a blessing. Plan ahead, prepare, gather or establish needed resources. Be wise and reasonable.

Likewise, the wives should be independent and self sufficient. Polygamy is expensive and demanding. It will take effort by all members to make it work. Income, time, and energy are key to making polygamy work better and produce a better lifestyle than monogamy. For individuals, these three items seldom coexist. In polygamy they may, especially if birthrates are kept in check. In religious polygamy the church wishes to bolster its numbers and encourages members to have many children. However, nothing can be more demanding than having too many children and too few attempting to keep them while others work to feed the expanding family. Keep the numbers and ages in balance. Do not have children until arrangements within the family have been made for their care and wellbeing. Have respect for society as a whole and do not have children to increase the amount of a welfare check. It gives others a bad reputation deserved by only a few.

There are good points if the group pulls together. In a study of early Mormon women by Dr. Vicky Burgess-Olson we read: "When the husbands were away visiting other wives in other houses, the wives they left behind ran farms, ranches or silkworm operations, and were literally heads of households. If the families shared the same house, the women had different assignments and could usually do what they liked best. Not being stuck with so much of the housework freed them for things like going to concerts or church. Of the sister wives studied, 54 percent had full-time jobs outside the home." Dr. Burgess-Olson goes on to say: I studied 341 pioneer Mormon women who shared 104 husbands. Just like today's marriages, some were happy, some weren't. But the idea that polygamist wives were necessarily jealous of each other is false. Some 91 percent of the wives I studied gave consent for the second and further marriages. Often it was the woman who suggested, "Maybe we'd better take another wife," and sometimes the first wife gave the subsequent bride away at the wedding.

Still, some wives objected. One disgruntled wife sent all the kids into the parlor, where her husband was courting his newest.

The writings of the wives indicated how they wished their husbands were around more, saying how cold their beds had gotten. We do know polygamist wives had fewer, but healthier, children than monogamous wives.

Most women went through a period of adjustment to having another woman share her husband. But then they would describe how they had "overcome jealousy" and were happy. There is a great deal of evidence that these women genuinely came to love each other. They celebrated birthdays together and wrote poetry to one another. One of them talked about the enjoyment of being a member of a family with three other wives and only having to deal with the husband one week a month. The women had fewer but healthier babies." Yet, the women complained in their diaries of "cold beds" and of missing their husbands."
(End Quote)

Of all complaints, "a cold bed," that is loneliness, lack of sexual fulfillment within the state of continued intimacy, and lack of resources is repeated throughout failed and failing polygamous relationships. Count the cost before entering in. Do not let this happen to you or your spouses.

Never sow jealousy, envy, or insecurity and as far as possible never allow it to be sown. Let all members be equal in love, service, and supply. Demand from members equal investment and commitment. Let no Machiavellian maneuvers or manipulations begin within the family. Jealousy, envy, and strife will poison the family. Communications should be free flowing within the confines of family meetings with the spouses having civil, mature conversations. Time should be allotted for discussions and plans.

Peace and harmony are a difficult aim but they can be maintained, most of the time.

U.S. State Laws

U.S. laws vary widely from state to state in regard to bigamy (being legally married to more than one living spouse,) co-habitation (living together without becoming legally married,) adultery (being married to one person while having sex with another,) and fornication (having sex without being married to that person). As the courts took on the task of legislating morality it found the need to plug any loophole it could find that led to any activity outside the template of the socially accepted ways.

According to the group, "U.S. Marriage Laws," states fall into various categories when it comes to marriage laws.

All 50 states have statutes against bigamy (multiple licensed marriages). In most states, bigamy is a felony.

In the following states, bigamy is a misdemeanor.
Alaska
Arkansas
Hawaii (petty misdemeanor-- 30 days in jail)
Iowa
Maine

Missouri

Montana

Nebraska

New Jersey

Ohio

Pennsylvania

Rhode Island (misdemeanor,$1000)

Tennessee

Texas

The following states, have **no** statutes against fornication, adultery, or cohabitation, and they also do not recognize common-law marriages.

California

Hawaii

Nevada

Oregon

Washington

The following states have statutes that concern adultery, but none for fornication, cohabitation, or common-law marriage. In some of them adultery is grounds for divorce only. In others the offending spouse simply forfeits any rights to the innocent spouse's estate. In the rest of them, adultery is a crime that can only be prosecuted by the offended spouse. In a successful polygamous relationship, these need not be obstructive. If the relationship fails, however, the statutory adulterer could be charged.

Connecticut

Delaware

Indiana

Kentucky

Louisiana

Maine

Maryland (Adultery results in a $10 fine and is grounds for divorce)

Missouri

New Jersey

Ohio

South Dakota

Tennessee

Texas (Texas **does** recognize common-law marriages, but apparently only if they are registered with the county clerk)

Vermont

Georgia and Illinois make adultery and fornication misdemeanors, although in Illinois the conduct must be "open and notorious."

The following states have laws against cohabitation.

Alabama

Alaska

Arkansas

Florida

Massachusetts

Mississippi

Nebraska

North Carolina

South Carolina

Virginia

West Virginia

Wyoming

The following states recognize common-law marriages or else make adultery a felony.

Colorado

Idaho

Iowa

Kansas

Montana

Oklahoma

Pennsylvania

Rhode Island

Utah

Washington D.C.

Wisconsin

Countries where polygamy is legal (including those where it is legal but limited):

Afghanistan, Algeria, Bahrain, Bangladesh, Brunei, Burkina Faso, Cameroon, Chad, Comoros, Congo, Djibouti, Egypt, Ethiopia, Gabon, The Gambia, India, Indonesia, Iran, Iraq, Jordan, Kuwait, Libya, Malaysia, Maldives, Mali, Mauritania, Morocco, Myanmar, Niger, Oman, Pakistan, Palestine, Qatar, Saudi Arabia, Senegal, Singapore, Somalia, South Africa, Sri Lanka, Sudan, Syria, Tanzania, Togo, Uganda, United Arab Emirates, Western Sahara, Yemen, Zambia.

Celibacy

Like much of the practice of polygamy, the practice of celibacy is driven by religious conviction. Yet, within the Bible, the foundational book used as a guideline for practices, there are instructions regarding polygamy and warnings against celibacy. Celibacy, according to the bible, is to be permitted for a married person only under certain circumstances and only for brief periods of time. Yet, Paul tells us some are suited for a life of celibacy, gaining peace and spiritual insight from the practice, being able to shift the energies and desires toward a deeper spiritual quest.

1 Timothy 4 (New International Version)
1 The Spirit clearly says that in later times some will abandon the faith and follow deceiving spirits and things taught by demons. 2 Such teachings come through hypocritical liars, whose consciences have been seared as with a hot iron. 3 They forbid people to marry and order them to abstain from certain foods, which God created to be received with thanksgiving by those who believe and who know the truth. 4 For everything God created is good, and nothing is to be rejected if it is received with thanksgiving, 5 because it is consecrated by the word of God and prayer.

Matthew 8 (New International Version)
14 When Jesus came into Peter's house, he saw Peter's mother-in-law
lying in bed with a fever. 15 He touched her hand and the fever left
her, and she got up and began to wait on him.

So, if the Catholic Church is correct and Jesus did tap Peter for the job of running the church or carrying forth the faith after He was killed, then Jesus designated Peter, a married man, to be the first pope. We will forego the discussion of who was actually running the show after the death of Jesus. It was, by the way, James who was the heir apparent, and not Peter. But we will leave that for another day.

Priests had married in Judaism. The priesthood itself was usually a hereditary profession, and it would seem that Christ accepted this part of the tradition in his choice of Peter.

To be fair, in that day and time, Paul believed that due to the need of travel and the likelihood of martyrdom it was best if those spreading the Gospel didn't have a family. Paul did go on to mandate that bishops, elders and deacons be only "the husband of one wife." This was because polygamy among all ranks of the clergy persisted. Supporting a large family with many wives did not leave time or energy for the ministry. By the third century bishops were required to be monogamous.

There were certain pressures within the early church. Some were political and driven out of greed. Some were religious in nature.

Of the religious pressures were the teachings of the Gnostic Christians, which caused great focus on the evils of the flesh. Spirit and the material world were at odds in their theology. Thus, the idea was that what starved the flesh of its natural desires must also feed the spirit. Neoplatonism was alive and well, and a major influence in the life and beliefs of Augustine.

Neoplatonism was the dominant philosophy of the ancient pagan world from the time of Plotinus in the mid-third century A.D., to the closing of the schools of philosophy at Athens by the Christian emperor Justinian in A.D. 529. It incorporated the best of Aristotle, Pythagoras, Plato, and the Stoics, so as to make a synthesis of the collected wisdom of the ancient world. Neoplatonism was not only a philosophy; it also met a religious need by showing how the individual soul might reach God. Thus it presented with traditional Greek rationalism a scheme of salvation comparable with those schemes offered by Christianity and the Mystery religions. It also began to influence Christian thinkers, notably Augustine.

Before receiving the final push from Augustine, the change in the church's views on marriage began with the Council of Elvira in Spain in about 306 A.D., which prohibited bishops, deacons and priests from marrying.

Already in 305 A.D., before the Church's liberation under Constantine, the Council of Elvira in Spain passed the following decree: "That bishops, priests and deacons, and in general all the clergy, who are specially employed in the service of the altar, abstain from conjugal intercourse. Let those who persist be degraded from the ranks of the clergy" (Can. 33). And by the end of the fourth century, the Second Council of Carthage in Africa declared, "What the apostles taught in the early Church preserved, let us too observe." Celibacy, I insist, is not a post factum afterthought of the Church. It is an anti factum, reality, practiced by the Church and wanted by those who wanted to be Christ's priests."

But this was influenced only partially by pagan philosophies. A political storm of greed was building.

Shortly after The Council of Elvira, the early church fathers began to stigmatize sex as sinful in their writings. St. Ambrose (340-397 A.D.) wrote, "The ministerial office must be kept pure and unspoiled and must not be defiled by coitus," and the former libertine, and some would argue – former sex addict, St. Augustine (354-430 A.D.) even went so far as to consider an erect penis a sign of man's insubordination.

Let us remember, Augustine was fighting his own demons in this arena. Certainly there will be times, if one is an addict, that total abstinence is easier than moderation, but for those who have normal drives, the suppression of normal human drives usually gives way to corruption and re-direction of those drives. It may be from this simple statement that pedophilia and homosexuality within the priesthood arises.

Augustine thought, "spontaneous sexual desire is...the clearest evidence of the effects of original sin."

Augustine concluded that human government, (and this certainly included the church,) were an indispensable defense against the forces of sin. This, we assume, was because government of any sort sets limitations, rules, and punishments for actions it deems unsuitable. But this is nothing more than replacing the Old Testament law with man's law. The latter will work no better than the first. It is a change of heart that is needed, not a change of taskmasters.

In every instance Augustine talks about sex, he implies that it was wrong or at least the reasons for having sex were wrong. However, it seems that he takes this belief a little too far. Maybe this stemmed from his studying with the Manichees and their belief that the body was the cause of evil. Maybe it stemmed from his interpretation of Catholicism and the Bible. Truly, Augustine is the first writer to show a change from a liberal view of sex to an extremely conservative view of sex and to argue the benefits that he believed it brought him. Even though his book is clearly Catholic propaganda, he shows himself as a lost sheep found, a reformed sinner; and that is a powerful message for many people. Like any good fundamental preacher of any faith, he knew that if something were good for his addictive personality it must be good for and forced upon all people. In short, Augustine believed the devil was not in the details, but lived in his pants. The equation of sin with sex is evident throughout Augustine's writing.

"I intend to remind myself of my past foulnesses and carnal corruptions, not because I love them but so that I may love you, my God" (Augustine, 24).

From his birth in a North African town, Augustine knew the religious differences overwhelming the Roman Empire: his father was a pagan who honored the old Punic gods; his mother was a zealous Christian. But the adolescent Augustine was consumed with sex and high living, and not with God.

At age 17, Augustine set off to school in Carthage in North Africa. There the underachiever became enraptured with his studies and started to make a name for himself. He immersed himself in the writings of Cicero and Manichaean philosophers and rejected his mother's religion.

His studies completed, Augustine returned to his home town of Thagaste to teach rhetoric Manichaeism. The philosophy was based on the teachings of the Persian, Mani, and was a dualist corruption of Christianity. It taught that the world of light and the world of darkness constantly war with each other, catching most of humanity in the struggle. Along with the religion of Zoroastrianism, these two religions influenced the dualistic outlook of Christianity the most. Augustine tried to hide his views from his mother, Monica, but when she found out, she threw him out of the house.

Augustine moved to Rome and there he began attending the cathedral to hear preaching of Ambrose the bishop. He kept attending because of Ambrose's preaching. He soon dropped his Manichaeism in favor of Neoplatonism, the philosophy of both Roman pagans and Milanese Christians.

His mother finally caught up with him and decided to find her son a proper wife. Augustine had a concubine he deeply loved, who had given him a son, but he would not marry her because it would have ruined him socially and politically.

Some believe that the conjunction of the emotional strain of grief in abandoning his lover along with the shift in philosophies left Augustine in a mode of self-loathing, which centered on his sexuality, which he saw as the blame for his pain. He attempted to renounce sex. For years he had sought to overcome his fleshly passions and nothing seemed to help. Becoming hypersensitive regarding the least of transgressions, he would reflect even on prepubescent tricks. Writing about the pear stealing of his youth, he reflected, "Our real pleasure consisted in doing something that was forbidden. The evil in me was foul, but I loved it." The self-loathing reformed sex addict over-compensated and became unstable, yet, the writings of Augustine would shape the church in time to come.

With the advent of the Dark Ages around 500, the upheavals in society saw a decline in clerical discipline and with it, a return to marriage and even the keeping of concubines by priests. During this time, the wealth of the church was also increasing, a development not lost on Rome. Many priests were leaving church lands to their heirs, and others handed down land of their own through primogeniture.

Now, this may not have been such a big deal if it weren't for the fact that priests were becoming wealthy. A priest or bishop would inform someone with land and means that they might burn in hell for their actions (or inactions). But perhaps they could be absolved if they left their lands to the Church. The duke or earl or baron would sign over a portion of his land or funds to the cleric in return for Salvation.

The bishops were leaving these acquisitions to their heirs. So the families of the bishops were becoming wealthy and powerful, the heads of State were losing revenues from taxes and the church was losing an opportunity to become the richest nation on Earth.

In 1018 A.D., Pope Benedict began to get serious about the matter when he decreed that descendants of priests could not inherit property.

Let us take a step back and follow the money. If a family had 2 or more sons it was customary to send one into the military or political arena and the other (usually the second son) into the clergy. When the father died the inheritance would be divided between the sons. If the church could stop the cleric from gaining a family, the church would inherit his worldly goods at the death of the cleric. When the priests balked at celibacy the pope found another way to steal the inheritance by proclaiming the families of clerics could not inherit, but instead the church would take over his land and money.

The Second Lateran Council finally made celibacy a law of the Church in 1139 A.D. Pope Gregory VII, who had assumed vast power by declaring himself the supreme authority over all souls, went even further by forbidding married priests from saying mass; he also forbade parishioners from attending masses said by them. Scholars believe that the first written law forbidding the clergy to marry was finally handed down at the Second Lateran Council in 1139 A.D.

The matter was brought up again in the 16th century, when dissenters tried to return to original Church doctrine, but the Council of Trent finalized the doctrine of celibacy in 1563 and the law finally became official doctrine at the Council of Trent in 1563.

In spite of all evidence showing the suppression of normal drives causes corruption and re-direction of such drives into deviant behavior, Rome's position on the issue has remained unchanged.

Money and land trump pedophilia and sexual abuse every time.

Just as a matter of curiosity, would it not be interesting to know if the popes that were so "motivated" to make celibacy for clergy mandatory actually followed their own orders? After all, if this command really was a holy order from on high the pope should also obey. But if it were a grab for power and riches then usually the head thief is above the law.

According to Wikipedia and other sources, there have been 265 popes. Many of them were sexually active within their papacy. Some were gay. There are various classifications for those who were sexually active at some time during their life. Periods in parentheses refer to the years of their papacies.

Married before receiving Holy Orders -
It was within canon law, and still is, for priests to have once been married before receiving Holy Orders. In the Eastern Rite branches of the Catholic Church, it is within canon law to be a priest and married (but one may not marry after ordination).

Their example of this is Saint Peter (Simon Peter), whose mother-in-law is mentioned in the Bible as having been miraculously healed (Matthew 8:14-15, Luke 4:38, Mark 1:29-31). According to Clement of Alexandria (Stromata, III, vi, ed. Dindorf, II, 276), Peter was married and had children and his wife suffered martyrdom. In some legends dating from at least the 6th century, Peter's daughter is called Petronilla.

Pope Clement I wrote, "For Peter and Philip begat children; [..] When the blessed Peter saw his own wife led out to die, he rejoiced because of her summons and her return home, and called to her very encouragingly and comfortingly, addressing her by name, and saying, 'Remember the Lord.' Such was the marriage of the blessed, and their perfect disposition toward those dearest to them."

Pope St. Hormisdas (514–523) was married and widowed before ordination. He was the father of Pope St. Silverius.

Pope Adrian II (867–872) was married, before taking orders, and had a daughter.

Pope John XVII (1003) was married before his election to the papacy and had three sons, who all became priests.

Pope Clement IV (1265–1268) was married, before taking Holy Orders, and had two daughters.

Pope Honorius IV (1285–1287) was married before he took the Holy Orders and had at least two sons. He entered the clergy after his wife died, the last pope to have been married.

Sexually active only before receiving Holy Orders -

Pope Pius II (1458–1464) had at least two illegitimate children (one in Strasbourg and another one in Scotland), born before he entered the clergy.

Pope Innocent VIII (1484–1492) (got to love that name) had at least two illegitimate children, born before he entered the clergy. According to the 1911 Encyclopaedia Britannica, he "openly practised nepotism in favour of his children." Girolamo Savonarola chastised him for his worldly ambitions.

Pope Clement VII (1523–1534) had one illegitimate son before he took holy orders. Some sources identify him with Alessandro de' Medici, Duke of Florence but this identification has not been confirmed.

Pope Gregory XIII (1572–1585) had an illegitimate son before he took holy orders.

Sexually active after receiving Holy Orders -

Pope Julius II (1503–1513) had at least one illegitimate daughter, Felice della Rovere (born in 1483, twenty years before his election). Some sources indicate that he had two additional illegitimate daughters, who died in their childhood.[16] Besides, some contemporary (possibly libellous) reports accused him of sodomy. According to the schismatic Council of Pisa in 1511, he was a "sodomite covered with shameful ulcers."

Pope Paul III (1534–1549) held off ordination in order to continue his promiscuous lifestyle, fathering four illegitimate children (three sons and one daughter) by his mistress Silvia Ruffini. He broke his relations with her ca. 1513. There is no evidence of sexual activity during his papacy. He made his illegitimate son Pier Luigi Farnese the first Duke of Parma.

Pope Pius IV (1559–1565) had three illegitimate children before his election to the papacy.

Sexually active during their pontificate -
Along with other complaints, the activities of the popes between 1458 and 1565, helped encourage the Protestant Revolt.

Pope Sergius III (904–911) was supposedly the father of Pope John XI by Marozia, according to Liutprand of Cremona in his

Antapodosis, as well as the Liber Pontificalis. However it must be noted that this is disputed by another early source, the annalist Flodoard (c. 894-966), John XI was brother of Alberic II, the latter being the offspring of Marozia and her husband Alberic I. Hence, John too may have been the son of Marozia and Alberic I. Bertrand Fauvarque underlines that the contemporary sources backing up this parenthood are dubious, Liutprand being "prone to exaggeration" while other mentions of this fatherhood appear in satires written by supporters of the late Pope Formosus.

Pope John X (914–928) had romantic affairs with both Theodora and her daughter Marozia, according to Liutprand of Cremona in his Antapodosis: "The first of the popes to be created by a woman and now destroyed by her daughter". (See also pornocracy)

Pope John XII (955–963) (deposed by Conclave) was said to have turned the Basilica di San Giovanni in Laterano into a brothel and was accused of adultery, fornication, and incest (Source: Patrologia Latina). The monk chronicler Benedict of Soracte noted in his volume XXXVII that he "liked to have a collection of women." According to Liutprand of Cremona in his Antapodosis, "they testified about his adultery, which they did not see with their own eyes, but nonetheless knew with certainty; he had fornicated with the widow of Rainier, with Stephana his father's concubine, with the widow Anna, and with his own niece, and he made the sacred palace into a whorehouse." According to The Oxford Dictionary of Popes, John XII was "a Christian Caligula whose crimes were rendered particularly horrific by the office he held". He was killed by a jealous husband while in the act of committing adultery with the man's wife. This was the era of pornocracy.

Pornocracy or the Rule of the Prostitutes/Rules of the Harlots or the more polite *Saeculum obscurum*, the Dark Age, which began in 904 AD with the installation of Pope Sergius III. The Pope was completely under the control of Theodora, the beautiful wife of Roman consul Theophylactus, who used sex to wield power. Theodora's 15-year-old daughter Morazia became the concubine of Pope Sergius III. Their son later became Pope John XI. Their illegitimate son later became Pope himself.

The era of Pornocracy ended with Pope John XII (the grandson of Marozia) in 963.

Pope Benedict IX (1032–1044, again in 1045 and finally 1047–1048) was said to have conducted a very dissolute life during his papacy. He was accused by Bishop Benno of Placenta of "many vile adulteries and murders."

Pope Victor III referred in his third book of Dialogues to "his rapes, murders and other unspeakable acts. His life as a Pope so vile, so foul, so execrable, that I shudder to think of it."

It prompted St. Peter Damian to write an extended treatise against sex in general, and homosexuality in particular. In his Liber Gomorrhianus, St. Peter Damian recorded that Benedict "feasted on immorality" and that he was "a demon from hell in the disguise of a priest", accusing Benedict IX of routine sodomy and bestiality and was said to have sponsored orgies.

In May 1045, Benedict IX resigned his office to pursue marriage, selling his office for 1,500 pounds of gold to his godfather, the pious priest John Gratian, who named himself Gregory VI.

Pope Alexander VI (1492–1503) had a notably long affair with Vannozza dei Cattanei before his papacy, by whom he had his famous illegitimate children Cesare and Lucrezia. A later mistress, Giulia Farnese, was the sister of Alessandro Farnese, who later became Pope Paul III. He fathered a total of at least seven, and possibly as many as ten illegitimate children.[40] (See also Banquet of Chestnuts)

Suspected to have been sexually active with male lovers -
Pope Paul II (1464–1471) was alleged to have died of a heart attack while in a sexual act with a page boy.

Pope Sixtus IV (1471–1484) was alleged to have awarded gifts and benefices to court favorites in return for sexual favors. Giovanni Sclafenato was created a cardinal by Sixtus IV for "ingenuousness, loyalty,...and his other gifts of soul and body",according to the papal epitaph on his tomb. According to Stefano Infessura, in his Diarium urbis Romae, he had a predilection for young boys.

Pope Leo X (1513–1521) was alleged to have had a particular infatuation for Marc-Antonio Flaminio.

Pope Julius III (1550–1555) was alleged to have had a long affair with Innocenzo Ciocchi del Monte. The Venetian ambassador at that time reported that Innocenzo shared the pope's bedroom and bed. According to the The Oxford Dictionary of Popes, he was "naturally indolent, he devoted himself to pleasurable pursuits with occasional bouts of more serious activity."

Continuing with our fun facts, according to "futurechurch.org" here is a list of popes who were the sons of the supposedly asexual clergy.

Popes who were the sons of other popes or other clergy –

Name of Pope	Papacy	Son of
St. Damascus I	366-348	St. Lorenzo, priest
St. Innocent I	401-417	Anastasius I
Boniface	418-422	son of a priest
St. Felix	483-492	son of a priest
Anastasius II	496-498	son of a priest
St. Agapitus I	535-536	Gordiaous, priest
St. Silverus	536-537	St. Homidas, pope
Deusdedit	882-884	son of a priest
Boniface VI	896-896	Hadrian, bishop
John XI	931-935	Pope Sergius III
John XV	989-996	Leo, priest

The same source supplied the following list of popes who had children out of wedlock AFTER the celibacy decree was in force.

Popes who had illegitimate children after 1139

Innocent VIII	1484-1492	several children
Alexander VI	1492-1503	several children
Julius	1503-1513	3 daughters
Paul III	1534-1549	3 sons, 1 daughter
Pius IV	1559-1565	3 sons
Gregory XIII	1572-1585	1 son

Why all this attention to clerics and the church? It goes toward a central point. Of all the martial statuses and modes, celibacy is the most accepted and the most dangerous. The number of priests convicted of pedophilia is both astonishing and disgusting. The fact that they are allowed to continue in their office as priests speaks to the church's indifference at best and conspiracy of like minds at worst. It also speaks to the unnaturalness of celibacy. Granted, there are a few people who find celibacy tolerable and fewer who find it preferable. It has been said that if one can adjust to celibacy ones life becomes more focused and less challenging. They are to be applauded. However, to force celibacy on those who are not predisposed to that way of life is to repress urges so deep and driving that they must erupt in unnatural or uncontrollable ways.

Many times, men who may be fighting aberrant sexual urges seek out the position of celibate priest in order to hide from their dragons, hoping God and church will help them control their drives. This is bound to fail. Then, there are those who seek out the priesthood in order to freely feed their desires.

Priests are just people like you and I. If a person desires to be celibate for the right reasons and has no problems keeping that commitment, let them go forth and enjoy the simplicity and focus it brings. Let it be a personal choice and not one thrust upon anyone by any church. No institution should have the power to contort and control something so basic, deep, and natural as a person's healthy sexual expression.

When Celibacy is a choice, and done for the correct reason, it can be a very healing time. Just as the bible suggests that we keep ourselves apart for a season so that we may more appreciate one another, extended acts of celibacy can heal wounds and renew souls.

I recently interviewed a lady in her 50's who had been celibate for several years. This is her story in her own words.

"Celibacy is not for everyone. However for some of us it is freeing and healing. After an abusive marriage of 9 tumultuous years I made a decision to remain celibate until marriage or a lifetime relationship came along. It was not a spur of the moment decision but a well thought out commitment. A commitment to myself. A celebration of life, a celebration of me.

No, I was not afraid of men or marriage. I simply needed time to see if I was still the same woman I had known myself to be before the abuse started. And if I was, I wanted to get to know her again. This was not; I repeat, not a religious game plan. And no it was not difficult, did not require fasting and constant groveling and praying. I prayed once and asked God to hide me and be my companion.

These are a few of the things that happened. I laughed more, a lot more. I enjoyed being alone. Who knew? And there was peace. The kind of internal peace that can't be explained.

I found out God is fun, and exceedingly funny. God was and is protective of me yet at the same time He empowered me. And I found that lady I was looking for. Me. I was so pleased to find out I was the woman I had known myself to be.

I began to feel worthwhile. I was able to celebrate life again. Simple day-to-day life became a joy.

Alone was not lonely. It was like coming alive again. Like spring at the end of a long, icy winter.

I regained my honor, dignity and strength. Those are the very things an abusive relationship can take from us. The very commodities we hope marriage or a good relationship will bring to our lives is what a bad relationship can and will destroy. I learned that those qualities needed for a good relationship have to be within each of us before the relationship begins.

I feel whole now. Free love and promiscuity can't do that for us. Nor can abusive, drama filled relationships. Sometimes we are our own counselors and healers. We just need to have the chance to get to know ourselves.

Did I mention I was celibate and didn't date for over 10 years ? A decision I've never regretted. "

(End interview)

Conclusion

Whether one chooses a life of celibacy, monogamy, polygyny, polyandry, or polyamory, it should be a personal choice, not a choice of the state or federal government. We may use the excuse of protecting children and weak willed adults but it does not hold water when one looks at the amount of spousal abuse committed within the common monogamous marriages of today.

Certainly, we should enforce rules of marital age. Possibly we should increase the minimum age of marriage in all states to eighteen. Certainly, we should protect the abused and neglected. But we should do these things for all types of marriages.

The more free will a person has the more likely the person can find their own happiness. Whether a person is gay, lesbian, a monogamist or polygamist, what difference does it make if love is found, nurtured, shared, and practiced?

First, do no harm, but then let the human spirit be free. Happiness and love will be the result.